Science K
Student Guide

Part 1

K12
A Stride Company

At Stride, Inc. (NYSE: LRN) – formerly K12 Inc. – we are reimagining lifelong learning as a rich, deeply personal experience that prepares learners for tomorrow. Since its inception, Stride has been committed to removing barriers that impact academic equity and to providing high-quality education for anyone—particularly those in underserved communities. The company has transformed the teaching and learning experience for millions of people by providing innovative, high-quality, tech-enabled education solutions, curriculum, and programs directly to students, schools, the military, and enterprises in primary, secondary, and post-secondary settings. Stride is a premier provider of K–12 education for students, schools, and districts, including career learning services through middle and high school curriculum. Providing a solution to the widening skills gap in the workplace and student loan crisis, Stride equips students with real world skills for in-demand jobs with career learning. For adult learners, Stride delivers professional skills training in healthcare and technology, as well as staffing and talent development for Fortune 500 companies. Stride has delivered millions of courses over the past decade and serves learners in all 50 states and more than 100 countries. The company is a proud sponsor of the Future of School, a nonprofit organization dedicated to closing the gap between the pace of technology and the pace of change in education. More information can be found at stridelearning.com, K12.com, destinationsacademy.com, galvanize.com, techelevator.com, and medcerts.com.

978-1-60153-328-9

Printed by Bradford & Bigelow, Newburyport, MA, USA, May 2021.

Table of Contents

Student Guide
Lesson 1: Observing My World

Scientists make careful observations of the world around them, but you don't have to be a scientist to explore your surroundings. Learn about your five senses and the sensing organs associated with each. Discover the properties of common objects by using appropriate sensory descriptors such as high and low, sweet and sour, and smooth and rough.

Lesson Objectives

- Explore concepts to be addressed during the year in Science K.
- Explain that a scientist observes.
- Name the five senses.
- Describe your observations, using one sense at a time.

PREPARE

Approximate lesson time is 45 minutes.

Advance Preparation

- It's important that you read the Course Introduction for Science K before your student begins the course. You can find the course introduction at the beginning of the Observing My World lesson.
- It's important that you read the course introduction for Science Kindergarten before starting this lesson. You can find it by clicking the OLS "Help" section.
- Prepare an observation game for this science lesson. Place a hammer, screwdriver, wrench or pliers, magnifying lens, scissors, ruler, paper, crayon, pencil, and glue stick on your work surface and cover them with a sheet or blanket. During the lesson your student will touch, taste, smell, or listen to the objects and guess what they are.

Materials

For the Student

crayons, 16 or more

glue sticks

pencils, no. 2

sheet - or blanket

tools - hammer, pliers, etc.

magnifying glass

paper, 8 1/2" x 11"

ruler, metric

scissors, round-end safety

My Senses

My Five Senses by Aliki (ISBN 006445083X)

paper, 8 1/2 x 11"

Five Senses

paper, colored construction, 12"x12"

stapler

Optional

"The Five Senses (It's Science)" by Sally Hewitt

Keywords and Pronunciation

observe : To notice something by using your senses. You *observe* the aroma of apple pie by using your sense of smell.

scientist : A person who asks many questions and uses careful observation to figure out how the world works. Scientists often do experiments in order to figure things out.

senses : The way that animals and humans learn about the outside world. Humans have five senses: sight, sound, smell, taste,and touch.

LEARN
Activity 1: Welcome to Science K *(Online)*

Activity 2: Scientific Observations *(Online)*

Activity 3: Tools for Observation *(Online)*

Activity 4: The Five Senses *(Online)*
Safety
Caution your student never to taste anything that is part of a Science lesson unless you have told him it is safe to do so.

Activity 5. Optional: Touching on Senses *(Online)*

ASSESS

Lesson Assessment: Observing My World (*Online*)

You will complete an offline assessment covering the main objectives of this lesson. Your learning coach will score this assessment.

LEARN

Activity 6. Optional: More About the Five Senses *(Online)*

Name   Date
_____   _____

My Senses

Circle the part of your body that you use to see.

Circle the part of your body that you use to hear.

Circle the part of your body that you use to touch.

Circle the part of your body that you use to taste.

Circle the part of your body that you use to smell.

Five Senses

Create your own Five Senses Booklet.

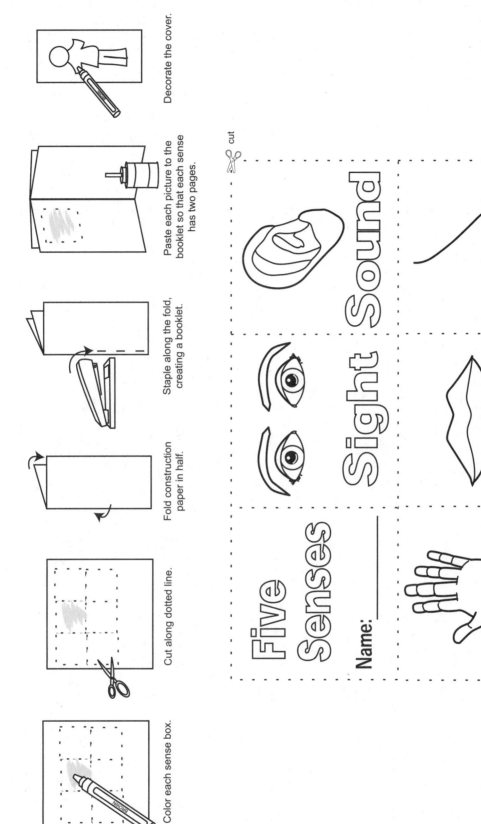

Decorate the cover.

Paste each picture to the booklet so that each sense has two pages.

Staple along the fold, creating a booklet.

Fold construction paper in half.

Cut along dotted line.

Color each sense box.

cut

Sound

Sight

Smell

Taste

Touch

Five Senses

Name: _____

Lesson Assessment

Observing My World

Short-Answer Question:

1. What are scientists doing when they look closely at things?
2. Name the five senses.
3. Choose an object you observed during the lesson with your sense of touch. Tell what it felt like.

Student Guide
Lesson 2: A Closer Look

Lesson Objectives

- Describe the function of eyes.
- Explain that light is needed in order for our eyes to see.
- Compare observations of small objects with and without a magnifying glass.

PREPARE

Approximate lesson time is 45 minutes.

Advance Preparation

- Prepare a scavenger hunt for this science lesson. Print Scavenger Hunt! and tape, glue, or staple the picture list of the scavenger hunt items to the side of a small paper bag. Out of your student's sight, hide all of the scavenger hunt items in one room before the lesson. Hide a few objects in dark locations, where your student will have to use his flashlight to find them. Your student should be able to find all of the items in five to ten minutes.

Materials

For the Student

My Five Senses by Aliki (ISBN 006445083X)

Scavenger Hunt!

bags, brown paper grocery

crayons, 16 or more - brown

glue sticks

leaf - green

lid, jar

mirror

flashlight

magnifying glass

markers, colored, 8 or more - green

paper clips - large

paper, 8 1/2" x 11"

penny

popsicle sticks

spoon - plastic

Magnifiers Make Things Look BIGGER

paper clips

Keywords and Pronunciation

magnify : To make something appear larger than it is so you can observe it more easily. If you magnify an ant under a magnifier, the ant looks much bigger than it really is.

LEARN
Activity 1: My Five Senses *(Online)*

Activity 2: Scavenger Hunt *(Online)*

Activity 3: Magnifiers Make Things Look BIGGER *(Online)*

Activity 4. Optional: A Close Review *(Online)*

ASSESS

Lesson Assessment: A Closer Look (*Online*)

You will complete an offline assessment covering the main objectives of this lesson. Your learning coach will score this assessment.

LEARN
Activity 5. Optional: I Spy *(Online)*

Activity 6. Optional: Fingerspelling *(Online)*

Name _____   Date _____

Scavenger Hunt!

penny

paperclip

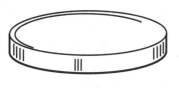

jar lid

brown crayon

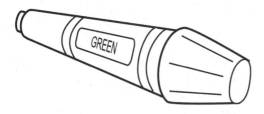

green marker

green leaf

plastic spoon

Popsicle stick

Name _____   Date _____

Magnifiers Make Things Look Bigger

Look through the magnifying glass and draw what you see.

leaf	paperclip
popsicle stick	**my choice**

Lesson Assessment

A Closer Look

Short-Answer Question:

1. Why do you use your eyes in Science?
2. Why can't you see in the dark?
3. How do things look when you observe them with a magnifying glass and without a magnifying glass?

Student Guide
Lesson 3: Sort by Sight

Lesson Objectives
- Sort objects according to their size, shape, and/or color.
- Describe objects by using the sense of sight.

PREPARE

Approximate lesson time is 45 minutes.

Materials

For the Student

    ball, rubber - any size

        Supermarket Spy

    blanket

    play equipment - baseball bat

    potted plant or houseplant

    toys - teddy bear

    bags, brown paper grocery - from scavenger hunt

    crayons, 16 or more - brown

    leaf - green

    lid, plastic

    paper clips - small

    penny

    popsicle sticks

    household items (10)

LEARN
Activity 1: How Things Look *(Online)*

Activity 2: I Spy with My Little Eye *(Online)*

Activity 3: Scavenger Sort *(Online)*

Activity 4. Optional: Describing Words *(Online)*

ASSESS

Lesson Assessment: Sort by Sight (*Online*)

You will complete an offline assessment covering the main objectives of this lesson. Your learning coach will score this assessment.

LEARN

Activity 5. Optional: Memory Game *(Online)*

Activity 4. Optional: Describing Words *(Online)*

Name

Date

Supermarket Spy

Find and circle these items at the grocery store.

Shopping List

Lesson Assessment

Sort or Sight

Short-Answer Question:

1. Use your senses to describe your favorite toy.
2. What do you see when you look into a mirror?
3. Name two things that are brown and two things that are red.
4. Think back to the Investigation activity when you sorted objects. What were the three ways you used to sort objects?

Student Guide
Lesson 4: Hear Here

Lesson Objectives
- Identify the parts of the body that we use for hearing.
- Describe sounds as loud or soft.
- Describe sounds as high or low.

PREPARE

Approximate lesson time is 45 minutes.

Materials
For the Student

 My Five Senses by Aliki (ISBN 006445083X)

 blindfold

  Sounds

 crayons, 16 or more

 glue sticks

 scissors, round-end safety

Optional

 pencils, no. 2

 paper, 8 1/2" x 11"

 glasses, drinking

 jars, baby food

 spoon

 water, tap

LEARN
Activity 1: What Do You Hear? *(Online)*

Activity 2: What's That Animal? *(Online)*

Activity 3: What's That Sound? *(Online)*

Activity 4. Optional: Sounds Around Us *(Online)*

ASSESS

Lesson Assessment: Hear Here *(Online)*

You will complete an offline assessment covering the main objectives of this lesson. Your learning coach will score this assessment.

LEARN

Activity 5. Optional: Glass Symphony *(Online)*

Safety

Ask your student to tap the jars gently to avoid breaking the glass.

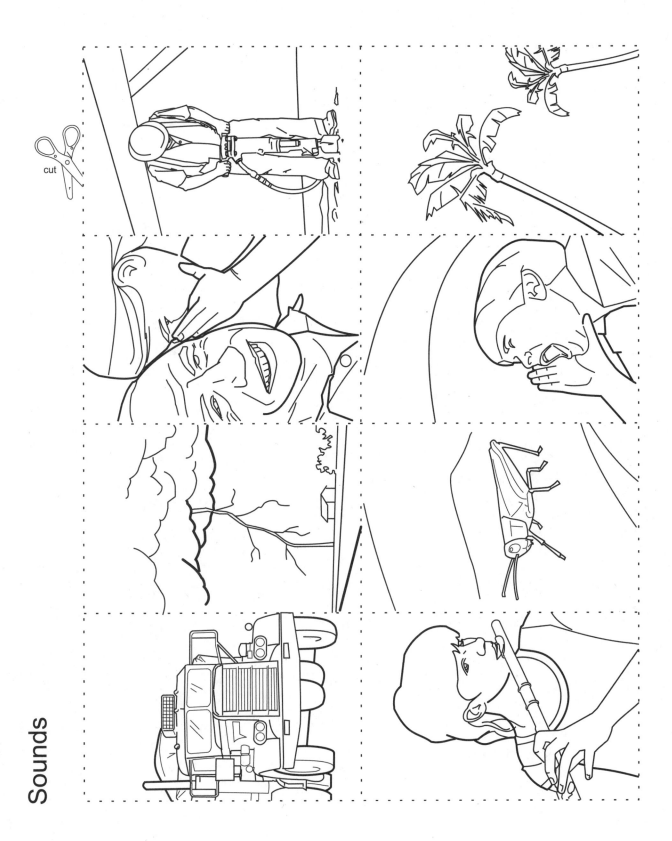

Sounds

Name _____ Date _____

Lesson Assessment

Hear Here

Short-Answer Question:

1. Point to the parts of your body that you use to hear.
2. Describe a loud sound.
3. Describe a high sound.
4. Describe a sound you like to listen to that is very soft or low.
5. Describe a sound you do not like to listen to that is very loud.

Student Guide
Lesson 5: Something Smells

Lesson Objectives
- Name the body part we use for smelling.
- Identify odors using the sense of smell.
- Explain that odors travel through the air.

PREPARE

Approximate lesson time is 45 minutes.

Advance Preparation
- For today's Science lesson, prepare four bags of strong-smelling items on which your student will test his sense of smell. Without your student's knowledge, place the following into bags: pieces of an onion, pieces of lemon peel, some popcorn, and a cotton ball sprayed with perfume. Fold down the tops of the bags so he can't see or smell the contents.

Materials
For the Student
- My Five Senses by Aliki (ISBN 006445083X)
- bag, brown paper, lunch (4)
- cotton balls
- vegetables - onion pieces
- fruits - lemon peel
- household items - perfume
- popcorn, popped (20)
- crayons, 16 or more
- household items - spray perfume, air freshener, vinegar
- paper, 8 1/2" x 11"
- vegetables - onion skin
- Elmer's Glue-All
- fruits - lemon peels

Optional
- cooking equipment - mixing bowl, oven
- cooking ingredients - cream of tartar, flavored extract, flour-3 cups
- salt - 1 1/2 cups
- vegetable oil - 3 tablespoons
- household items - perfumed oil
- water, tap - 3 cups

Keywords and Pronunciation

odor : A fragrance or smell. Some odors are pleasant, such as the odor of flowers, and some odors are unpleasant, such as that of burnt toast.

LEARN
Activity 1: Reviewing the Five Senses *(Online)*

Activity 2: What's That Smell? *(Online)*
Safety
This lesson involves eating or using food. Before beginning, check with your doctor, if necessary, to assess whether your student will have any allergic reaction to this food.

Demonstrate to your student the safe way to smell something unknown: Open the container and gently wave your hand across the top to push the air toward your nose. Never place your nose close to an item and inhale deeply.

Activity 3: The Speed of Smell *(Online)*

Activity 4: The Pleasant and the Unpleasant *(Online)*

Activity 5. Optional: A Sense of Smell *(Online)*

ASSESS
Lesson Assessment: Something Smells (*Online*)
You will complete an offline assessment covering the main objectives of this lesson. Your learning coach will score this assessment.

LEARN
Activity 6. Optional: Smelly Dough *(Online)*

Lesson Assessment

Something Smells

Short-Answer Questions:

1. Point to the part of your body that you use to smell.
2. How are you able to identify items in a bag without being able to see, hear, taste, or feel them?
3. Why can you smell fresh-baked cookies in the kitchen if you are standing in a different room?
4. Name something that is pleasant to smell and something that is unpleasant to smell.

Student Guide
Lesson 6: You've Got Taste

Lesson Objectives

- Explain the function of the tongue and taste buds.
- Identify foods using the sense of taste.
- Compare sweet and sour tastes.

PREPARE

Approximate lesson time is 45 minutes.

Advance Preparation

- For this Science lesson, place bite-sized pieces of lemon, chocolate, potato chips, cheese, and banana on separate paper plates out of your student's sight. Prepare another plate for the second activity with the following food samples: two jelly beans, a small cup of lemonade, two pieces of dill pickle, two red grapes, a small cup of fruit punch, and two lemon-drop candies.
- Gather a few old magazines with food pictures that your student can cut out.

Materials

> For the Student
>
>> My Five Senses by Aliki (ISBN 006445083X)
>>
>> mirror - small
>>
>> blindfold
>>
>> candy - chocolate
>>
>> cheese
>>
>> crayons, 16 or more
>>
>> cups, plastic
>>
>> plates, paper (5)
>>
>> potato chips
>>
>> fruits - banana, lemon
>>
>> water
>>
>> candy - jellybeans, lemon drops (2)
>>
>> crayons, 16 or more - assorted colors
>>
>> food - dill pickle (2)
>>
>> fruit drink - lime, grape
>>
>> fruits - grapes (2)
>>
>> paper, 8 1/2" x 11"
>>
>> magazines
>>
>> Elmer's Glue-All
>>
>> scissors, round-end safety
>
> Optional
>> Lentil by Robert McCloskey

Keywords and Pronunciation

taste buds : Groups of bumps on the tongue that let us taste. Our taste buds tell us if something is sweet, sour, salty, or bitter.

LEARN
Activity 1: My Five Senses *(Online)*

Activity 2: What's that Taste? *(Online)*
Safety
This lesson involves eating food. Check with your doctor, if necessary, to assess whether your student will have any allergic reaction to this food.

Activity 3: Sweet or Sour? *(Online)*

Activity 4: Tastes We Like *(Online)*

Activity 5. Optional: Taste *(Online)*

ASSESS
Lesson Assessment: You've Got Taste (*Online*)
You will complete an offline assessment covering the main objectives of this lesson. Your learning coach will score this assessment.

LEARN
Activity 6. Optional: Pucker Up *(Online)*

Lesson Assessment

You've Got Taste

Short-Answer Questions:

1. What are the little bumps on your tongue called?
2. What do your tongue and taste buds do?
3. Name a sweet food and a sour food.
4. How are you able to identify different foods without being able to see them?

Student Guide
Lesson 7: A Touchy Subject

Lesson Objectives

- Categorize objects as hard, soft, rough, or smooth, using the sense of touch.
- Identify objects using only the sense of touch.
- Recognize that you can use multiple senses at the same time.

PREPARE

Approximate lesson time is 45 minutes.

Advance Preparation

- Before the lesson, gather 3" x 3" pieces of the following materials: sandpaper, silk, fake fur, facial tissue, aluminum foil, and colored construction paper. Crumple, then flatten, the aluminum foil. Glue uncooked rice to the piece of construction paper.

Materials

For the Student

    My Five Senses by Aliki (ISBN 006445083X)

    cotton balls

    facial tissue - 3" x 3"

    fake fur - 3" x 3"

    foil, aluminum - 3" x 3"

    paper, colored construction, 12"x12" - cut to 3" x 3"

    paper, newsprint, 8 1/2" x 11" or larger

    rock

    silk - 3" x 3"

    Elmer's Glue-All

    sandpaper - 3" x 3"

    ball, rubber

    crayons, 16 or more

    macaroni, dried - small handful

    tube socks (5)

    fork

    toothbrush

Optional

    Our Five Senses

    pencils, colored, 16 or more

    pencils, no. 2

    index cards, 4" x 6" (2)

    paper, 8 1/2" x 11" (2)

    tape, clear

Keywords and Pronunciation

texture : The feel of something, especially its roughness or smoothness. An eggshell has a smooth *texture*.

LEARN
Activity 1: The Sense of Touch *(Online)*

Activity 2: How Does It Feel? *(Online)*

Activity 3: What's in the Sock? *(Online)*

Activity 4: How Many Senses Can You Use? *(Online)*

Activity 5. Optional: It Makes Sense To Me *(Online)*

ASSESS
Lesson Assessment: A Touchy Subject (*Online*)

You will complete an offline assessment covering the main objectives of this lesson. Your learning coach will score this assessment.

LEARN
Activity 6. Optional: Fingerprints *(Online)*

Name _____   Date _____

Our Five Senses

Circle the body part that shows the sense being used.

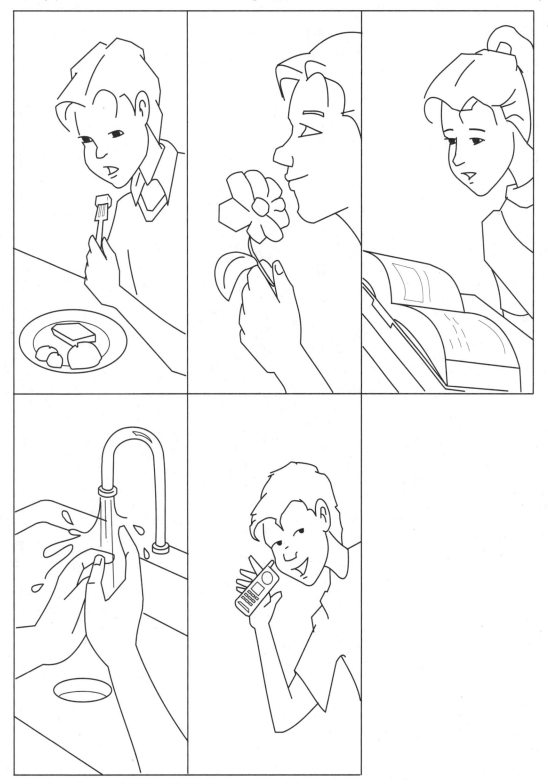

Name _____   Date _____

Lesson Assessment

A Touchy Subject

Short-Answer Question:

1. Find something in the room that feels smooth.
2. Find something in the room that feels rough.
3. What sense did you use to find out what things were in the sock?
4. Let's say you are at a parade. What two senses would you use to tell that there was a band playing and marching down the street?
5. How are you able to identify items in the socks without being able to see the items?

Student Guide
Lesson 1: Everybody's Bodies

Explore the amazing human body. Learn how our skeleton holds us up and gives us shape and how our muscles let us move. Find out how our heart pumps blood, how our brain controls our bodies and allow us to think and remember, and how our teeth tear and grind our food.

Lesson Objectives

- Identify and compare external features of the human body.

PREPARE

Approximate lesson time is 45 minutes.

Materials

For the Student

> You and Me Lab Sheet

crayons, 16 or more

mirror - full-length

scales

markers, colored, 8 or more

scissors, round-end safety

tape measure

Optional

string

tape, masking

paper, butcher

pencils, no. 2

LEARN
Activity 1: Our Bodies *(Online)*

Activity 2: You and Me *(Online)*

Activity 3. Optional: Alike and Different *(Online)*

ASSESS

Lesson Assessment: Everybody's Bodies *(Offline)*

You will complete an offline assessment covering the main objectives of this lesson. Your learning coach will score this assessment.

LEARN

Activity 4. Optional: The Real You *(Online)*

Name _____ Date _____

You and Me Lab Sheet

Fill in the blanks. Use a measuring tape and a scale to measure height and weight. Draw a portrait showing what you look like.

I have_____eyes.   I have_____hair.

I am_____tall.   I weigh_____pounds.

Name _____ Date _____

Lesson Assessment

Everybody's Bodies

Short-Answer Question:

1. Look at the picture you drew of yourself. Name five things in your picture that are the same on all people.
2. Name three things that are different between the two pictures you drew.
3. Point to two places on your picture that look the same.

Student Guide
Lesson 2: Bones Make Our Skeletons

Lesson Objectives

- Explain that our skeletons hold us up and give us shape.
- Recognize that bones fit together at the joints to make our skeletons.
- Explain that bones protect the insides of our bodies.
- Identify major joints of the body.

PREPARE

Approximate lesson time is 45 minutes.

Materials

For the Student

     Skeleton Match-Up

glue sticks

pencils, no. 2

scissors, round-end safety

Optional

chicken bone

jar - large, glass with lid

vinegar - 240 ml

Keywords and Pronunciation

joint : A place where two bones meet. Your knuckles are *joints* between your finger bones.

skeleton : The framework of bones that supports and protects our bodies. Your *skeleton* is made up of more than 200 bones.

LEARN
Activity 1: What's on the Inside? *(Online)*

Activity 2: Bones of All Shapes and Sizes *(Online)*

Activity 3. Optional: Bones Give You Shape *(Online)*

ASSESS
Lesson Assessment: Bones Make Our Skeletons (*Online*)

You will complete an offline assessment covering the main objectives of this lesson. Your learning coach will score this assessment.

LEARN
Activity 4. Optional: Rubber Bones (*Online*)

Name   Date

Skeleton Match-Up

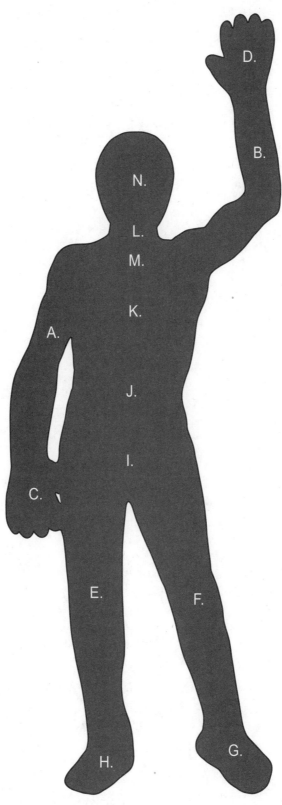

Skeleton Match-Up

Cut out the bones one at a time and glue them on the other page in the space with the matching letter.

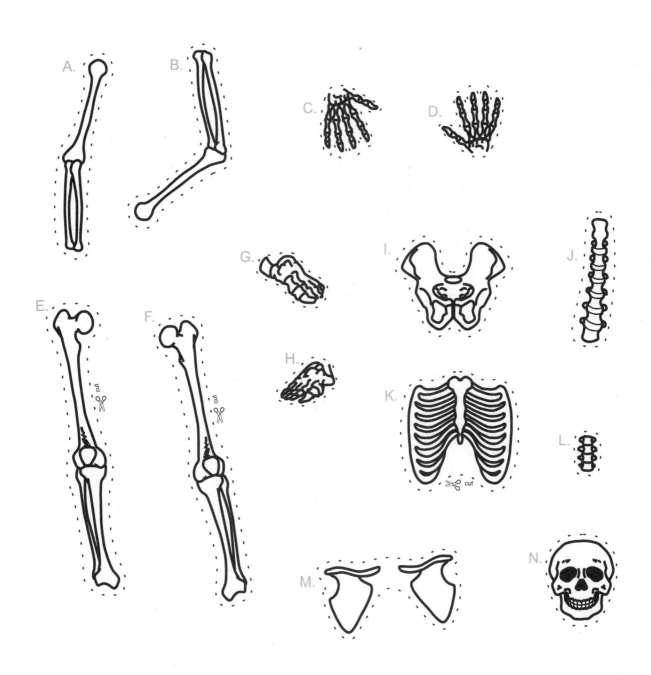

Name _____ Date _____

Lesson Assessment

Bones Make Our Skeletons

Short-Answer Question:

1. Our bodies move and bend at places where two bones meet. Are these places called *joints* or *skills*?
2. Simon says, "Point to your elbow." Is your elbow a bone or a joint?
3. All your bones fit together at the joints. What do these bones make up?
4. Bones give us shape and hold us up. But what do bones protect?
5. What holds your body up and helps it keep its shape?

Student Guide
Lesson 3: Inside Out

Lesson Objectives

- Explain how muscles work.
- Explain that the heart pumps blood through the body.
- Know that the brain controls our bodies and allows us to think and remember.

PREPARE

Approximate lesson time is 45 minutes.

Advance Preparation

- If you don't have it already, you will need a paper towel tube and a toilet paper tube for the Inside Out lesson.

Materials

For the Student

Show Your Muscles!

balloons - deflated (2)

paper towel tube

tape, clear - four strips

toys - car

My Body

crayons, 16 or more

toilet paper tubes

toys

Optional

glue sticks

pencils, no. 2

scissors, round-end safety

Keywords and Pronunciation

brain : The part of your body inside your head that controls your body and allows you to think and remember. You use your brain to figure things out.

heart : The part of your body that pumps blood all through your body. You can't live if your heart stops beating.

muscle : A part of your body that helps you move. Your muscles get stronger when you exercise.

LEARN

Activity 1: Bones to Muscles *(Online)*

Activity 2: Show Your Muscles! *(Online)*

Activity 3: The Heart: The Strongest Muscle *(Online)*

Safety

Be sure that when your student takes his pulse at his neck he does not press too hard. Pressing hard can cause injury.

Activity 4: The Brain *(Online)*

Activity 5. Optional: My Body Review *(Online)*

ASSESS

Lesson Assessment: Inside Out (*Online*)

You will complete an offline assessment covering the main objectives of this lesson. Your learning coach will score this assessment.

LEARN

Activity 6. Optional: Use that Body *(Online)*

Name _____   Date _____

Show Your Muscles!

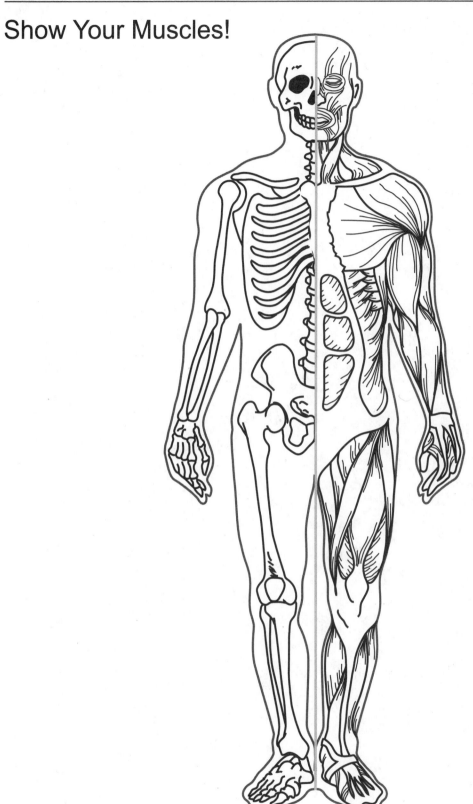

57

Name _____   Date _____

My Body

Cut out the clues at the bottom of the page and glue them next to the body part they describe. Use the Word Bank to help you write the name of each body part next to the matching clue.

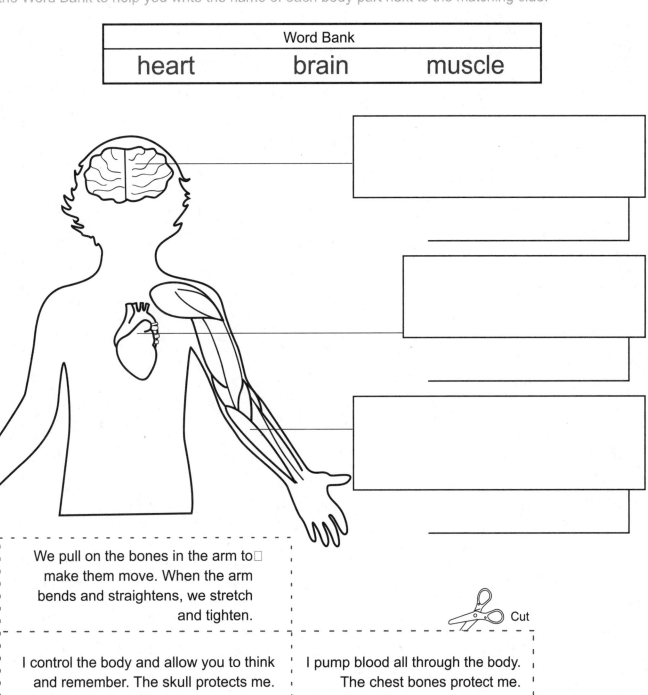

Word Bank		
heart	brain	muscle

We pull on the bones in the arm to☐ make them move. When the arm bends and straightens, we stretch and tighten.

✂ Cut

I control the body and allow you to think and remember. The skull protects me.

I pump blood all through the body. The chest bones protect me.

Name _____   Date _____

Lesson Assessment

Inside Out

Questions

    1.) Point to where your brain is located. What does your brain do?

    2.) What does your heart do?

    3.) What do your muscles do?

Student Guide
Lesson 4: A Toothy Grin

Lesson Objectives

- Explain that we use our front teeth to bite or tear food and our back teeth to grind and chew food.
- Identify the three main outer parts of the tooth: the crown, the neck, and the root.
- State that people are born with two sets of teeth.
- Explain ways to keep teeth healthy.

PREPARE

Approximate lesson time is 45 minutes.

Materials

For the Student

 mirror - small

 fruits - apple

  My Teeth

 crayons, 16 or more

 glue sticks

 scissors, round-end safety

Optional

 paper, 8 1/2" x 11"

 Open Wide: Tooth School Inside by Laurie Keller

LEARN
Activity 1: Teeth at Work *(Online)*

Activity 2: What Do Teeth Do? *(Online)*

Activity 3: Tooth Close-Ups *(Online)*
Safety

This lesson involves eating or using food. Check with your doctor, if necessary, to assess whether your student will have any allergic reaction to this food.

Activity 4: Healthy Teeth *(Online)*

Activity 5. Optional: All About Teeth *(Online)*

ASSESS

Lesson Assessment: A Toothy Grin (*Online*)

You will complete an offline assessment covering the main objectives of this lesson. Your learning coach will score this assessment.

LEARN

Activity 6. Optional: Open Wide *(Online)*

My Teeth

Cut out the names of the three main parts of a tooth at the bottom. Glue them where they belong next to the picture of the tooth.

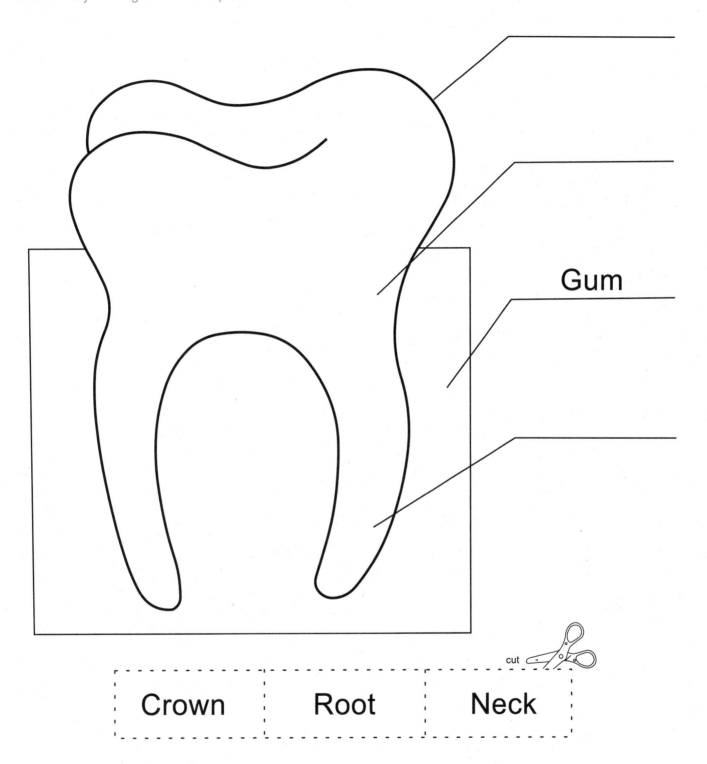

Gum

cut

Crown | Root | Neck

Lesson Assessment

A Toothy Grin

Questions

1.) What do we use our front teeth for?

2.) What do we use our back teeth for?

3.) Name some ways that you can keep your teeth healthy.

4.) Will you always have the same teeth that began growing in your mouth when you were a baby?

5.) Eating too much of what type of foods could make your teeth unhealthy?

6.) Point to the crown, neck, and root on this tooth.

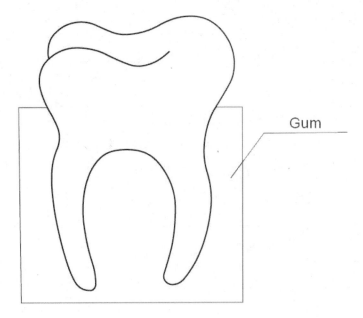

Gum

Student Guide
Lesson 1: What's Alive?

Our fascinating world consists of both living and nonliving things, and many living things are either plants or animals. Learn that plants and animals have some similarities and some differences, but they all need food, water, and air to grow. Find out why plants need sunlight and animals need shelter.

Lesson Objectives

- Determine whether something is living or nonliving.
- Know that living things grow with food, water, and air.

PREPARE

Approximate lesson time is 45 minutes.

Materials

> For the Student
>> What's Alive? by Kathleen Weidner Zoehfeld (ISBN 0-06-445132-1)
>> pencils, no. 2
>> paper, 8 1/2" x 11" (2)
> Optional
>> leaves - brown and green
>> magnifying glass

LEARN
Activity 1: What's Living and What's Not (Online)

Activity 2: What's Alive? (Online)

Activity 3: How Do You Know It's Alive? (Online)

Activity 4. Optional: What's Alive? Review (Online)

ASSESS

Lesson Assessment: What's Alive? (Online)

You will complete an offline assessment covering the main objectives of this lesson. Your learning coach will score this assessment.

LEARN
Activity 5. Optional: Draw Your Favorites (Online)

Lesson Assessment

What's Alive?

Questions:

1.) What things need food, water, and air?

2.) What question can we ask to find out if something is living?

3.) Is a rock living or nonliving? How do you know?

4.) Is an elephant living or nonliving? How do you know?

5.) Are all animals living things?

Student Guide
Lesson 2: What Do Plants Need?

Lesson Objectives

- Name the three main things that plants need: food, water, and air.
- State that plants use sunlight to make food.
- Know that plants take in water through their roots.
- Know that plants take in air through tiny holes in their leaves.

PREPARE

Approximate lesson time is 45 minutes.

Advance Preparation

- You will need a packet of radish seeds for this Science lesson.

- If you are completing this lab during a season where seeds are not available, you can purchase seeds from websites such as http://www.burpee.com.

Materials

For the Student

What Does a Plant Need?

What's Alive? by Kathleen Weidner Zoehfeld (ISBN 0-06-445132-1)

crayons, 16 or more

cardboard, boxes

cotton balls (24)

cups, plastic - 6 or 8 oz (4)

marker, black permanent, non-toxic - felt tip

household items - dishes- 3 small

seeds, radish - packet

toothpicks

water, tap

Optional

What Do Plants Need? Game Cards

scissors, round-end safety

Keywords and Pronunciation

nutrient : Something that plants need to stay strong and healthy. Soil and water contain nutrients, and plant roots take in water and nutrients.

LEARN

Activity 1: Is It Alive? *(Online)*

Activity 2: What Does a Plant Need? *(Online)*

Activity 3: A Seed's Needs, Part 1 *(Online)*

Activity 4. Optional: Reviewing What Plants Need *(Online)*

ASSESS

Lesson Assessment: What Do Plants Need? (*Online*)

You will complete an offline assessment covering the main objectives of this lesson. Your learning coach will score this assessment.

LEARN

Activity 5. Optional: Plant Scavenger Hunt *(Online)*

Name _____   Date _____

What Does a Plant Need?

Color the three things plants need.

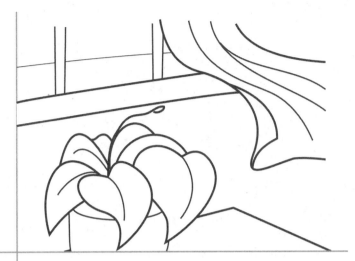

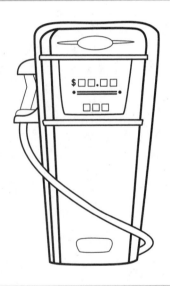

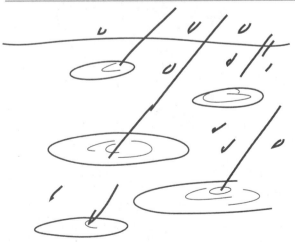

75

What Do Plants Need? Game Cards

Cut

Name _____ Date _____

Lesson Assessment

What Do Plants Need?

Questions:

1.) Why do plants need sunlight?

2.) What three things do plants need to live?

3.) How do plants get air?

4.) Plants take in water through their _____.

Student Guide
Lesson 3: What Do Animals Need?

Lesson Objectives
- Know how animals' needs are different from plants' needs.
- Know that shelter is a place where animals make their homes, in order to keep safe.
- Name the three main things that animals need: food, water, and air.
- Identify what animals eat and what they use for shelter.

PREPARE

Approximate lesson time is 45 minutes.

Materials
For the Student

What Do Animals Need?

What's Alive? by Kathleen Weidner Zoehfeld (ISBN 0-06-445132-1)

crayons, 16 or more

Optional

paper

Animal Homes by Tammy Everts and Bobbie Kalman

Elmer's Glue-All

shoeboxes

Keywords and Pronunciation
shelter : A place where animals make their homes and where they can be safe from danger. Sometimes, animals look for shelter when they are frightened.

LEARN
Activity 1: An Animal's Life *(Online)*

Activity 2: What Animals Need *(Online)*

Activity 3. Optional: Reviewing What Animals Need *(Online)*

ASSESS
Lesson Assessment: What Do Animals Need? (*Online*)

You will complete an offline assessment covering the main objectives of this lesson. Your learning coach will score this assessment.

LEARN
Activity 4. Optional: Animal Homes (*Online*)

Name _____   Date _____

What Do Animals Need?

Circle the answers about animal needs.

1. Circle the cow's shelter.

2. How does a frog get its food?

3. Where does a bird live?

Name _____ **Date** _____

What Do Animals Need?

Circle the answers about animal needs.

4. Which leaf did a caterpillar eat?

5. Circle the part of your body you use to breathe.

6. People are animals, too.
   Circle what animals need to live.

Lesson Assessment

What Do Animals Need?

Questions:

1. What are the three most important things that all animals need?
2. Can animals make their own food? Why or why not?
3. How does a shelter help an animal?
4. What does an animal have to do to find food that plants do not have to do?

Student Guide
Lesson 4: Changes

Lesson Objectives
- Identify how living things can grow and change.
- Identify how nonliving things can change.
- Conclude what happens to a plant when it does not get everything it needs to grow.

PREPARE

Approximate lesson time is 45 minutes.

Materials
For the Student

Things Change

crayons, 16 or more

paper, 8 1/2" x 11"

LEARN
Activity 1: Plants and Animals *(Online)*

Activity 2: Things Change *(Online)*

Activity 3: A Seed's Needs, Part 2 *(Online)*

Activity 4. Optional: Reviewing Changes *(Online)*

ASSESS

Lesson Assessment: Changes (*Online*)

You will complete an offline assessment covering the main objectives of this lesson. Your learning coach will score this assessment.

LEARN
Activity 5. Optional: I Can See the Future *(Online)*

Before	After

89

Lesson Assessment

Changes

Questions:

1.) How did the radish seeds in your investigation change when you gave them sunlight, air, and water?

2.) How does a pair of shoes change if you leave them outside?

3.) Can plants grow without water?

Student Guide
Lesson 1: Plant Structures

Discover some of the similarities and differences in a variety of plants. Find out how plants can grow from seeds and produce seeds in their fruit. Next, observe, sort, and graph different seed types. Examine some common edible plants and learn how to identify their structures.

Lesson Objectives
- Name the following plant structures: root, stem, trunk, branch, leaf, flower, and fruit.
- Compare plant structures among a variety of different plants.

PREPARE

Approximate lesson time is 45 minutes.

Advance Preparation
- Plant a sunflower seed three weeks before this Science lesson or buy a small house plant that you are willing to remove from its pot. If you want, you can save your radish plants from Unit 3 (Introduction to Living things) Lesson 2 (What Do Plants Need?) for the Learning About Plants activity. Don't forget to keep watering them.
- Just before the lesson, take the plant out of the pot and gently shake or rinse the soil from its roots. To remove the plant without damaging it, place your index finger and middle finger on each side of the stem at the soil level. While holding the pot with the rest of your hand, invert the pot and gently tap out the plant. The plant should fall out easily into your hand.
- A third option is to carefully pull up a weed with the roots intact.
- If you are completing this lab during a season where seeds are not available, you can purchase seeds from websites such as http://www.burpee.com.

Materials
For the Student
Build a Plant
Leaf and Flower Pattern
1-hole punch
crayons, 16 or more
paper towel tube
paper, colored construction, 12"x12" - green, yellow, and black
paper, heavy
paper, newsprint, 8 1/2" x 11" or larger
pot, plant - empty
potted plant or houseplant
seeds, sunflower (3)
brads

Elmer's Glue-All
magnifying glass
pipe cleaners
scissors, round-end safety
tape, clear

LEARN
Activity 1: What Plants Need *(Online)*

Activity 2: Learning About Plants *(Online)*
Safety
Pipe cleaners may have sharp ends. Handle them carefully.

Activity 3. Optional: Reviewing Plant Structures *(Online)*

ASSESS
Lesson Assessment: Plant Structures (*Offline*)
You will complete an offline assessment covering the main objectives of this lesson. Your learning coach will score this assessment.

LEARN
Activity 4. Optional: Sock Plants *(Online)*

Leaf and Flower Pattern

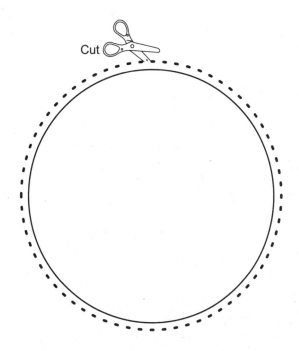

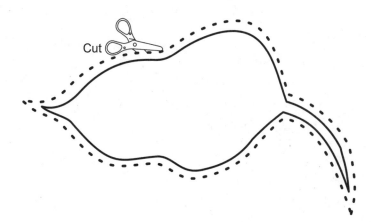

Leaf and Flower Pattern

Build A Plant

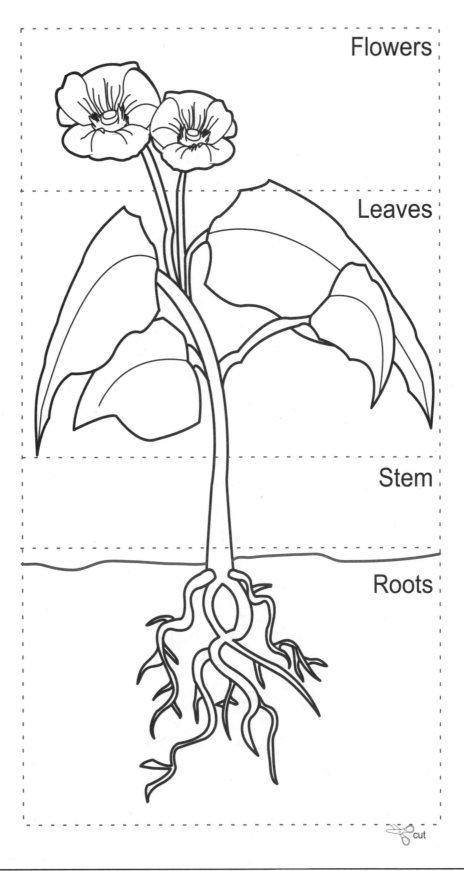

Flowers

Leaves

Stem

Roots

cut

Name _____

Date _____

Plant Structures Assessment

Color the stem of the tomato plant green. Color the roots of each plant brown. Color the leaves of each plant green. Color the fruit of each plant red. Color the trunk and branches of the apple tree gray.

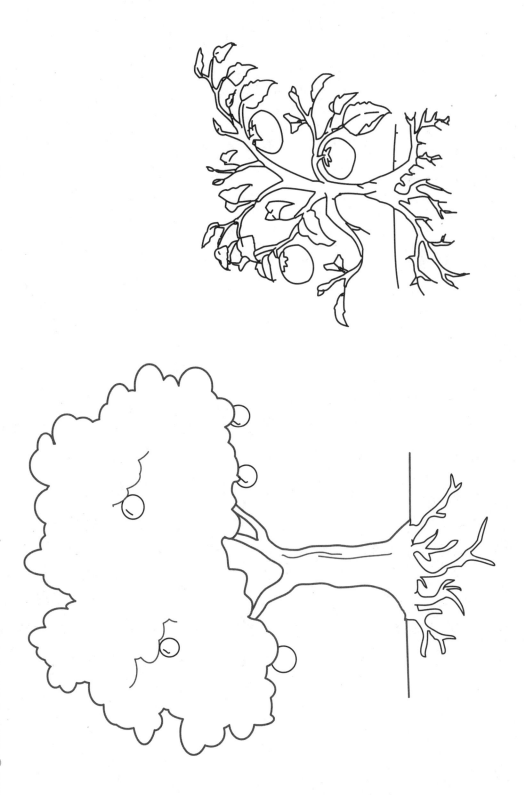

Student Guide
Lesson 2: Sow Many Seeds!

Lesson Objectives

- Recognize that there are many different types of seeds.
- Identify seeds and fruits that we eat.
- Compare, sort, and graph seed types by their physical attributes.
- State that the fruit is the part of the plant that contains seeds.

PREPARE

Approximate lesson time is 45 minutes.

Advance Preparation

- For this Science lesson, gather a variety of dried beans. You may wish to use a bean soup mix with several types of beans in one package. Also gather more unusual types of seeds, if possible, such as an avocado or peach pit, grass seeds, or mustard seeds. Have on hand several whole fruits and vegetables with seeds inside. Good examples to use are cucumbers, tomatoes, apples, oranges, kiwi, and green peppers, but other types are also acceptable.

Materials

    For the Student

        Seed Graph

      beans, dried - assorted varieties (10)

      crayons, 16 or more

      cup, paper (4)

      paper, colored construction, 12"x12"

      plates, paper

      seeds, corn (10)

      seeds, sunflower (10)

      Elmer's Glue-All

      magnifying glass

      seeds, radish (10)

      knife, kitchen - sharp

      vegetables - with seeds inside (2)

      fruits (2)

      paper, 8 1/2" x 11"

      scissors, round-end safety

Keywords and Pronunciation

flower : The part of the plant that develops before the fruit starts to grow. The fruit grows after the flower dies. Flowers bloom from the stem and often smell sweet.

fruit : The part of the plant that contains the seeds. Apples are the fruit of the apple tree.

seed : The part of a plant that can grow into a new plant. If you cut open an apple, you can see its *seeds*.

LEARN

Activity 1: Seeds *(Online)*

Safety

This lesson involves eating or using food. Before beginning, check with your doctor, if necessary, to assess whether your student will have any allergic reaction to this food.

Activity 2: Looking at Seeds *(Online)*

Activity 3: Where Are the Seeds? *(Online)*

Safety

Be careful when handling the knife and do not let your student use it.

ASSESS

Lesson Assessment: Sow Many Seeds! (*Online*)

You will complete an offline assessment covering the main objectives of this lesson. Your learning coach will score this assessment.

Name   Date

Seed Graph

Count your seeds. Color one box for each kind of seed.

10				
9				
8				
7				
6				
5				
4				
3				
2				
1				
glue seeds →				

Name _____ Date _____

Lesson Assessment

Sow Many Seeds!

Questions:

1. In what ways are seeds different from each other?
2. In what part of a plant would you find the seeds – the stem or the fruit?
3. Name two foods we eat that are seeds.

Student Guide
Lesson 3: Plants as Food

Lesson Objectives

- Identify plant roots, stems, leaves, flowers, and fruit as food that we eat.

PREPARE

Approximate lesson time is 45 minutes.

Advance Preparation

- For this Science lesson have on hand several samples of edible plants such as celery, broccoli, carrots, lettuce, and bananas. Try to find produce with as much of the entire plant structure intact as possible. For example, find carrots or radishes with the green leaves still attached. Other plants that you may use in place of carrots are beets, radishes, or turnips. Use spinach or cabbage in place of lettuce and cauliflower instead of broccoli.

- Grocery stores discard old produce and may give it to you free. If you use discarded produce, however, do not allow your student to eat any of it.

Materials

For the Student

      vegetables - lettuce, broccoli, carrots, celery, radishes, string beans

      fruits - bananas

      knife, kitchen - sharp

      paints, finger

      paper, colored construction, 12"x12" - white

      pencils, no. 2

      plates, paper (5)

      vegetables - cabbage, beans, carrots, celery, lettuce

Optional

      Fruit Salad and Vegetable Stew Review

      alum

      cloth - wool or cotton

      pan - stainless steel

      sieve

      soap, laundry

      vegetables - varieties

      bowl - glass

      fruits - blackberries

      water

Keywords and Pronunciation

flower : The part of the plant that develops before the fruit starts to grow. The fruit grows after the flower dies. Flowers bloom from the stem and often smell sweet.

fruit : The part of the plant that contains the seeds. Apples are the fruit of the apple tree.

seed : The part of a plant that can grow into a new plant. If you cut open an apple, you can see its *seeds*.

LEARN
Activity 1: Plants Help Us All *(Online)*
Safety
This lesson involves eating or using food. Before beginning, check with your doctor, if necessary, to assess whether your student will have any allergic reaction to this food.

Activity 2: What Part Do We Eat? *(Online)*

Activity 3: Plant Painting *(Online)*

Activity 4. Optional: Reviewing Plants as Food *(Online)*

ASSESS

Lesson Assessment: Plants as Food (*Online*)
You will complete an offline assessment covering the main objectives of this lesson. Your learning coach will score this assessment.

LEARN
Activity 5. Optional: Make Plant Dye *(Online)*

Name

Date

Fruit Salad and Vegetable Stew Review

Circle the fruits we eat. Underline the leaves we eat.
Draw a box around the roots we eat. Color the stems green.

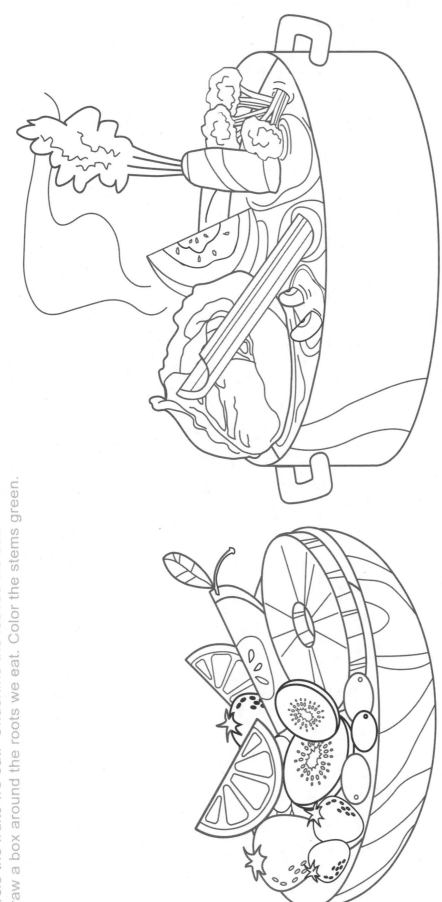

Name _____ Date _____

Lesson Assessment

Plants as Food

Questions:

1.) Name a fruit you have eaten.

2.) Name a plant that has roots that we eat.

3.) Name a plant that has leaves that we eat.

4.) Name a plant that has flowers that we eat.

5.) Name a plant that has stems that we eat.

Student Guide
Lesson 4: Trees Are Plants, Too!

Lesson Objectives

- Name the following parts of a tree: root, trunk, branch, twig, leaf, and bark.
- State that deciduous trees lose their leaves in the fall and grow new ones in the spring.
- State that evergreen trees keep their leaves all year round.

PREPARE

Approximate lesson time is 45 minutes.

Materials

> For the Student
>> crayons, 16 or more
>> paper, 8 1/2" x 11" - white
>
> Optional
>> Trees, Please!
>
> leaves - several
> paper, 8 1/2" x 11"
> bottle, plastic
> cloth - white, T-shirt
> hammer
> vinegar
> wood block - thin
> "The Giving Tree" by Shel Silverstein

Keywords and Pronunciation

deciduous (dih-SIH-juh-wuhs) : Having leaves that fall off during certain seasons or at a certain developmental stages. In the fall we rake up the leaves from deciduous trees.

deciduous trees : Trees that lose all their leaves in the fall and grow new ones in the spring. The maple is a *deciduous tree* whose leaves turn red and yellow in the autumn.

evergreen trees : Trees that keep their leaves all year round. An *evergreen tree* will still have green leaves in the winter.

LEARN
Activity 1: Eating Plants *(Online)*

Activity 2: The Many Faces of Trees (*Online*)

Activity 3. Optional: Reviewing Trees (*Online*)

ASSESS

Lesson Assessment: Trees Are Plants, Too! (*Online*)

You will complete an offline assessment covering the main objectives of this lesson. Your learning coach will score this assessment.

LEARN

Activity 4. Optional: Leaf Rubbings (*Online*)

Activity 5. Optional: Leaf Print Shirts (*Online*)

Activity 6. Optional: The Giving Tree (*Online*)

Name _____   **Date** _____

Trees, Please!

Deciduous: Spring

Deciduous: Fall

Evergreen: Spring

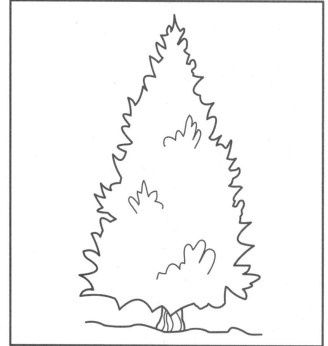

Evergreen: Fall

Name _____   Date _____

Lesson Assessment

Trees Are Plants Too!

1. What kind of trees lose their leaves in the fall and grow new ones in the spring?

2. What kind of trees have leaves that stayed green all year round?

3. In the space below draw a tree. Label the root, trunk, branch, twig, leaf, and bark of the tree.

4. What is the covering on the outside of the tree called?

Student Guide
Lesson 1: What's That Animal?

Explore the wonderful variety of animals on our planet. Examine their fur, feathers, skin, and other body coverings, and find out how they move using different body parts. Recognize that some animals eat plants, some eat animals, and others eat both. Meet Jane Goodall, whose 10-year study of chimpanzees helped people gain a better understanding of animals.

Lesson Objectives

- Identify animal bodies and coverings including fur, feathers, scales, a hard outer shell, and smooth skin and soft bendable bodies.
- Match animals to their body coverings.

PREPARE

Approximate lesson time is 45 minutes.

Advance Preparation

- Print the Animal Coverings Mobile pattern sheet, glue it onto cardstock, and cut out the animals. Cut the pieces of fur into little pieces so you can glue them onto the pattern later. Use the hole punch to make holes near the top of each animal cutout. Unwind a wire clothes hanger, then shape it into a circle. Tie six pieces of string equidistant around the circle.

Materials

For the Student

Animal Coverings Mobile

candy - gummy worm

clay

crayons, 16 or more

cups, plastic - clear

fake fur

feathers, natural - 1 large, 6 small (7)

hanger, wire clothes

macaroni, dried - shell-shaped uncooked

beads - sequins

card stock (3)

Elmer's Glue-All

Play-Doh

scissors, round-end safety

yarn

Optional
> blanket
>> Animal Coverings Match
> pencils, no. 2

LEARN
Activity 1: Animal Body Coverings *(Online)*

Activity 2: Animal Cover-Up *(Online)*

Activity 3. Optional: Animal Coverings Match *(Online)*

ASSESS
Lesson Assessment: What's That Animal? (*Online*)

You will complete an offline assessment covering the main objectives of this lesson. Your learning coach will score this assessment.

LEARN
Activity 4. Optional: Pet the Animals *(Online)*

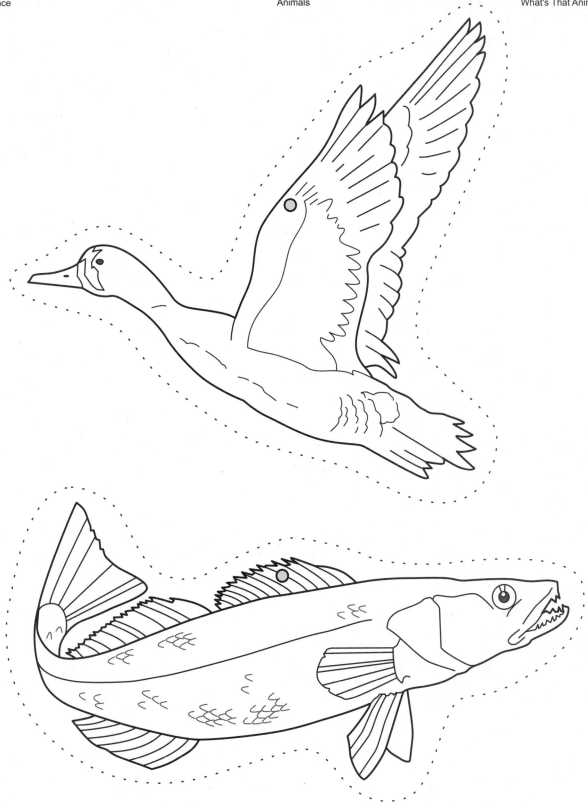

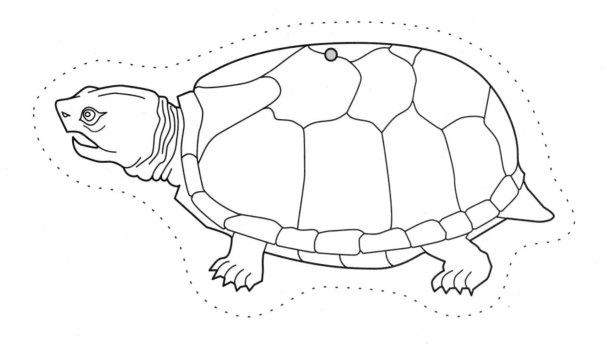

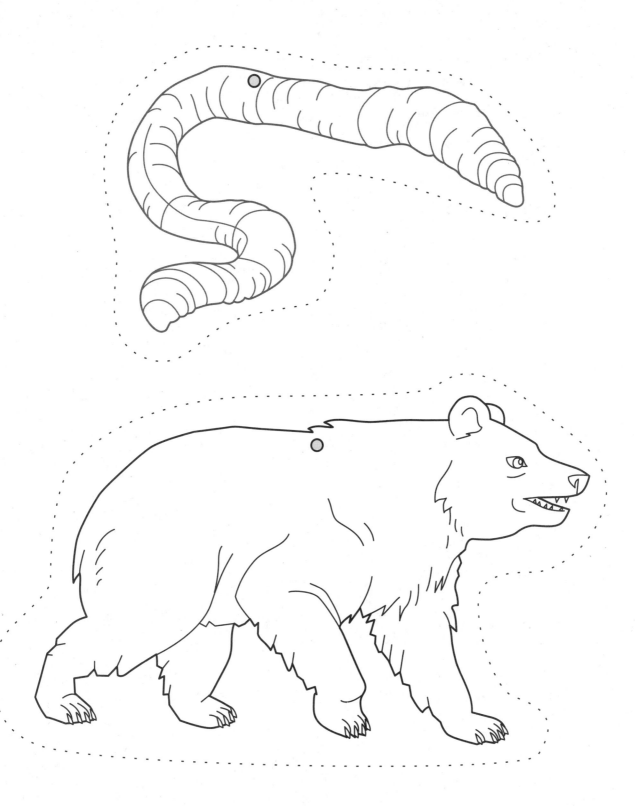

Name _____   Date _____

Animal Coverings Match

Name the animal on the left side and its type of body covering. Find an animal on the right side that has the same body covering. Draw a line from each animal on the left to the animal on the right that has a similar body covering.

Lesson Assessment

What's That Animal?

Questions:

1.) What type of animal has fur as a body covering?

2.) What type of animals has feathers as a body covering?

3.) Name an animal whose smooth skin and soft bendable body helps it move through the soil.

4.) What type of body covering does a fish have?

5.) What kind of body covering does a turtle have?

Student Guide
Lesson 2: Animal Motion

Lesson Objectives

- Identify how animals move.
- Match animal features that are used for movement.
- Demonstrate different types of animal movements.

PREPARE

Approximate lesson time is 45 minutes.

Materials

For the Student

Here's How I Move

crayons, 16 or more

magazines

toys - stuffed animals (6)

pencils, no. 2

index cards, 4" x 6" (8)

scissors, round-end safety

LEARN
Activity 1: Moving Along *(Online)*

Activity 2: How Animals Move *(Online)*

Activity 3: Sort the Animals *(Online)*

Activity 4. Optional: Review Moving Along *(Online)*

ASSESS

Lesson Assessment: Animal Motion (*Online*)

You will complete an offline assessment covering the main objectives of this lesson. Your learning coach will score this assessment.

LEARN
Activity 5. Optional: Animal Videos *(Online)*

Name _____   Date _____

Here's How I Move

Color the animals and circle the animal body part that helps the animal move.

Name _____   Date _____

Lesson Assessment

Animal Motion

Questions:

1.) Give an example of an animal that has legs.

2.) Give an example of an animal that swims.

3.) Give an example of an animal that has wings.

4.) Give an example of four different animals and then tell which body parts help them move.

5.) One at a time, show how four different animals move. What parts of their bodies do they use to move?

Student Guide
Lesson 3: What Do Animals Eat?

Lesson Objectives
- Know that some animals eat plants, others eat animals, and some eat both plants and animals.
- Identify how animals get their food.

PREPARE

Approximate lesson time is 45 minutes.

Advance Preparation
- If you choose to do the Optional Activity, Look at the Animals, collect several books with pictures of animals eating that clearly show what the animals are eating. Examples might be cows eating grass, a lion catching its prey, a monkey eating bananas, etc.

Materials
> For the Student
>> Who Eats What?
>>
>> crayons, 16 or more
>>
>> scissors, round-end safety
>
> Optional
>> glue sticks
>>
>> paper, heavy
>>
>> books - with pictures of animals

LEARN
Activity 1: What Do Animals Eat? *(Online)*

Activity 2: Animal Food *(Online)*

Activity 3. Optional: Reviewing Animal Meals *(Online)*

ASSESS

Lesson Assessment: What Do Animals Eat? (*Online*)

You will complete an offline assessment covering the main objectives of this lesson. Your learning coach will score this assessment.

LEARN
Activity 4. Optional: Look at The Animals (Online)

Name

Date

Who Eats What?

Cut out the animal pictures and glue them under the heading that matches the type of food the animal eats.

Name _____   Date _____

PLANTS	ANIMALS	BOTH

Name _____   Date _____

Lesson Assessment

What Do Animals Eat?

Questions:

1. What does a giraffe eat?

2. What does a lion eat?

3. What do bears eat?

4. Do all animals eat the same thing?

5. What does a giraffe use to get its food to its mouth?

6. What does an eagle use to get food to its mouth?

7. What does an elephant use to get food to its mouth?

Student Guide
Lesson 4: Biography: Jane Goodall

Lesson Objectives

- Explain that Jane Goodall studied animal behavior.
- Explain that Jane Goodall discovered that chimpanzees use tools.
- Observe animal behavior.

PREPARE

Approximate lesson time is 45 minutes.

Materials

For the Student

    penny

Optional

    crayons, 16 or more

    paper, heavy

Keywords and Pronunciation

animal behavior : What animals do and how they live. She recorded the *animal behavior* of the chimps.

observe : To watch something carefully. Jane Goodall *observed* the animals through the trees.

LEARN
Activity 1: Observing Behavior *(Online)*

Activity 2: Jane Goodall *(Online)*

Activity 3: Follow that Ant! *(Online)*

Activity 4: Watch that Bird! *(Online)*

Activity 5. Optional: Review Jane Goodall *(Online)*

ASSESS

Lesson Assessment: Jane Goodall (*Online*)

You will complete an offline assessment covering the main objectives of this lesson. Your learning coach will score this assessment.

LEARN
Activity 6. Optional: Be a Biologist (Online)

Lesson Assessment

Jane Goodall

Questions:

1. What is the name of the lady who lived in Africa and studied chimpanzees?

2. How did Jane Goodall find out that chimpanzees use tools?

3. When you watch an ant, a bird, or any other animal, what are you observing?

Student Guide
Lesson 1. Optional: Life in a Tree

This unit is OPTIONAL. It is provided for students who seek enrichment or extra practice.
Identify types of animals that make their homes in trees, ponds, and caves. Find out how these animals get food and shelter. Recognize that *nocturnal* animals are more active during the night and *diurnal* animals are more active during the day. Examine how nocturnal animals use their senses at night.

Lesson Objectives

- State that trees can provide homes for many animals.
- Identify ways animals use trees for food and shelter.

PREPARE

Approximate lesson time is 45 minutes.

Advance Preparation

- Use butcher paper or brown grocery bags to make a tree trunk approximately 3 feet tall. Tape the trunk to a door, the refrigerator door, or an empty wall. You can cut a flat shape or crinkle the paper to create a trunk with more "depth." You and your student will create the branches and leaves together during the lesson.

Materials

For the Student

    Leaf Patterns

    Life In a Tree

  crayons, 16 or more

  paper, colored construction, 12"x12" - green

  pencils, no. 2

  paper - brown butcher

  paper, 8 1/2" x 11"

  scissors, round-end safety

  tape, clear

Optional

  bags, brown paper grocery

    What Doesn't Belong?

    What Doesn't Belong? Key

  magnifying glass

  newspaper - or magazines

Keywords and Pronunciation

shelter : A place where animals can stay safe and protected from danger. The squirrel found shelter in the tree during the rainstorm.

LEARN
Activity 1. Optional: Optional Lesson Instructions *(Online)*

Activity 2. Optional: Trees as Homes *(Online)*

Activity 3. Optional: Life in a Tree *(Online)*

Activity 4. Optional: What Doesn't Belong? *(Online)*

Activity 5. Optional: Visit a Tree *(Online)*

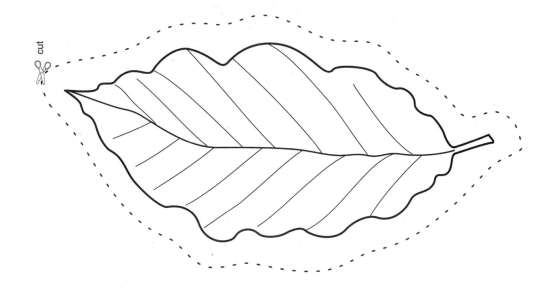

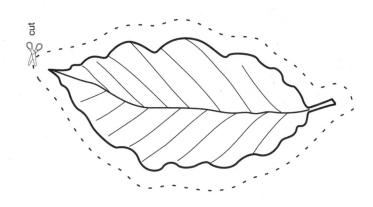

Leaf Patterns

153

cut

cut

cut

cut

cut

cut

Name _____   Date _____

What Doesn't Belong?

Draw an X on the things that don't belong in a tree.

Student Guide
Lesson 2. Optional: Life in a Pond

Lesson Objectives

- Identify animals and plants that make their homes in and around a pond.

PREPARE

Approximate lesson time is 45 minutes.

Materials

For the Student

    Pond Plants and Animals

crayons, 16 or more

glue sticks

paper, colored construction, 12"x12" - green, blue

rock - assorted small

twig - several

pipe cleaners

scissors, round-end safety

tape, clear

Optional

    What Doesn't Belong?

    What Doesn't Belong? Key

jar - with lid

pencils, no. 2

glass, drinking

paper, 8 1/2" x 11"

Keywords and Pronunciation

pond : A fairly shallow body of water that is smaller than a lake. The boy watched the ducks swim in the *pond*.

LEARN
Activity 1. Optional: Optional Lesson Instructions *(Online)*

Activity 2. Optional: Ponds Are Homes, Too *(Online)*

Activity 3. Optional: Pond Life *(Online)*

Activity 4. Optional: What Doesn't Belong? *(Online)*

Activity 5. Optional: Visit a Pond *(Online)*

Activity 2. Optional: Ponds Are Homes, Too *(Online)*

Pond Plants and Animals

cut

cut

cut

cut

cut

fold

fold

fold

cut
fold
cut
fold
cut
fold
cut
fold
cut
fold
cut
fold

Name _Ryker_   Date _11-9-21_

What Doesn't Belong?

Draw an X on the things that don't belong in a pond.

Student Guide
Lesson 3. Optional: Life in a Cave

Lesson Objectives

- Know caves can provide homes for many animals.
- Identify animals that use a cave for safety and shelter.

PREPARE

Approximate lesson time is 45 minutes.

Materials

For the Student

　　　　Cave Animals

　　　bags, brown paper grocery

　　　bottle, spray

　　　crayons, 16 or more

　　　glue sticks

　　　paper, colored construction, 12"x12" - blue

　　　card stock (2)

　　　scissors, round-end safety

　　　water

Optional

　　　What Doesn't Belong?

　　　What Doesn't Belong? Key

LEARN
Activity 1. Optional: Optional Lesson Instructions *(Online)*

Activity 2. Optional: Caves as Homes *(Online)*

Activity 3. Optional: Life in a Cave *(Online)*

Activity 4. Optional: What Doesn't Belong? *(Online)*

Activity 5. Optional: Cave Life *(Online)*

Activity 4. Optional: What Doesn't Belong? *(Online)*

Activity 5. Optional: Cave Life *(Online)*

Cave Animals

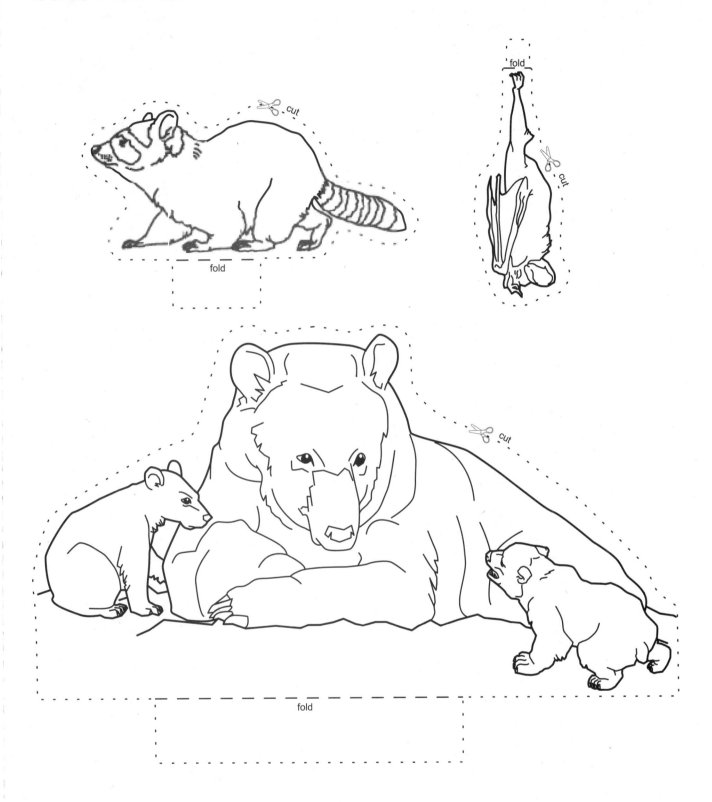

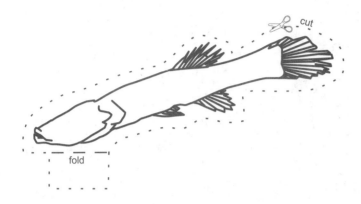

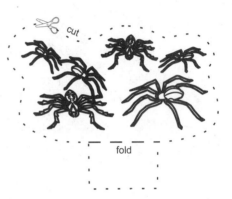

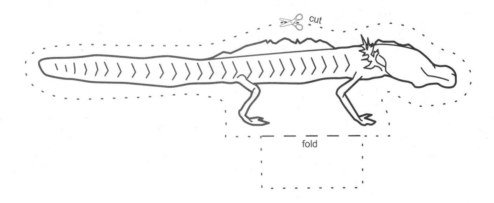

Name _____   Date _____

What Doesn't Belong?

Draw an X on the things that don't belong in a cave.

Student Guide
Lesson 4. Optional: Night Animals

Lesson Objectives

- Know that nocturnal animals are active mostly at night.
- Know that diurnal animals are active mostly during the day.
- Match nocturnal animals with the senses they use most to find their way in the dark.

PREPARE

Approximate lesson time is 45 minutes.

Advance Preparation

- If you don't already have it, you will need to gather the *Where Are the Night Animals?* by Mary Ann Fraser (New York: HarperTrophy, 1999) book for the optional lesson.

Materials

For the Student

"Where Are the Night Animals? "by Mary Ann Fraser (ISBN 0-06-445176-3)

Nocturnal Animals Use Their Senses

crayons, 16 or more

pencils, no. 2

Keywords and Pronunciation

diurnal (diy-UR-nuhl) : Animals that are more active during the day. The dog is *diurnal,* actively playing outside during the day and sleeping at night.

nocturnal (nahk-TUHR-nl) : Animals that are more active during the night. The bat is *nocturnal,* asleep throughout the day and active at night.

LEARN
Activity 1. Optional: Optional Lesson Instructions *(Online)*

Activity 2. Optional: Night Animals *(Online)*

Activity 3. Optional: Read "Where are the Night Animals?" *(Online)*

Activity 4. Optional: Nocturnal Sensing *(Online)*

Activity 5. Optional: Review "Where are the Night Animals?" *(Online)*

Activity 6. Optional: Nocturnal Animal Senses *(Online)*

Activity 7. Optional: Night Sight! *(Online)*

Name _____   Date _____

Nocturnal Animals Use Their Senses

Draw a line to match the nocturnal animals with the sense they use the most to find their way in the dark.

smell

sight

touch

hearing

Student Guide
Lesson 1: Length and Height

Learn how to use your senses and nonstandard units to measure objects. Practice these new skills by sequencing objects according to their weight, capacity, height, length, and temperature. Experiment with a thermometer to find out how you can use it to tell about temperature.

Lesson Objectives

- Explain that height is how high or tall something is.
- Explain that length is how long something is.
- Sequence a group of objects by their height or length.
- Compare the height and length of two objects.

PREPARE

Approximate lesson time is 45 minutes.

Materials

For the Student

     crayons, 16 or more

     glasses, drinking - different heights (5)

     mirror - full length

     pen, ballpoint

     pencils, no. 2

     twig - small

     toothpicks

Optional

     macaroni, dried - various shapes and sizes

Keywords and Pronunciation

height : How high or tall something is. The height of that building must be 100 feet tall.

length : The distance from one end of an object to the other. Look at the length of that snake!

size : The measurement of how large or small something is. The size of an ant is very different from the size of an elephant.

LEARN
Activity 1: The Size of It *(Online)*

Activity 2: Which Is Taller, Which Is Longer? *(Online)*

Activity 3. Optional: Draw to Compare *(Online)*

ASSESS

Lesson Assessment: Length and Height (*Online*)

You will complete an offline assessment covering the main objectives of this lesson. Your learning coach will score this assessment.

LEARN

Activity 4. Optional: Sort by Shape and Size *(Online)*

Name _____   Date _____

Lesson Assessment

Length and Height

Questions:

1. Name an object that is taller than you.

2. Name an object whose length is longer than a crayon's.

3. Which is taller - a mountain or a house?

4. Which is longer -- a crayon or an arm?

5. Find three of your favorite toys, or three different objects in the room. Put the three toys or objects standing up in order from tallest to shortest.

6. Find three objects in the room. Lay down the objects on their side and put them in order from longest to shortest.

Student Guide
Lesson 2: Give Me a Hand

Lesson Objectives

- Measure lengths in nonstandard units.
- Make a pictograph to compare the measurements of several objects in nonstandard units.

PREPARE

Approximate lesson time is 45 minutes.

Materials

For the Student

Give Me A Hand Pictograph

crayons, 16 or more

spoon

table - small

toys - stuffed animal

Optional

Measuring with Pennies

pencils, no. 2

penny (12)

book

paper, 8 1/2" x 11"

Keywords and Pronunciation

pictograph : A picture graph that shows information using picture symbols. The pictograph showed pictures of colored jelly beans to show the number of beans of each color.

LEARN
Activity 1: Comparing Sizes *(Online)*

Activity 2: How Many Hands Long? *(Online)*

Activity 3. Optional: Measuring With Pennies *(Online)*

ASSESS

Lesson Assessment: Give Me A Hand (*Online*)

You will complete an offline assessment covering the main objectives of this lesson. Your learning coach will score this assessment.

LEARN

Activity 4. Optional: More Measuring (*Online*)

Name _____   Date _____

Give Me a Hand Pictograph

Color the hands in the graph to represent the length of each object.

| book | small table | pillow | stuffed animal | spoon |

Name _____   Date _____

Measure With Pennies Review Sheet

Measure the length of these objects in pennies. Color the number of pennies above each item.

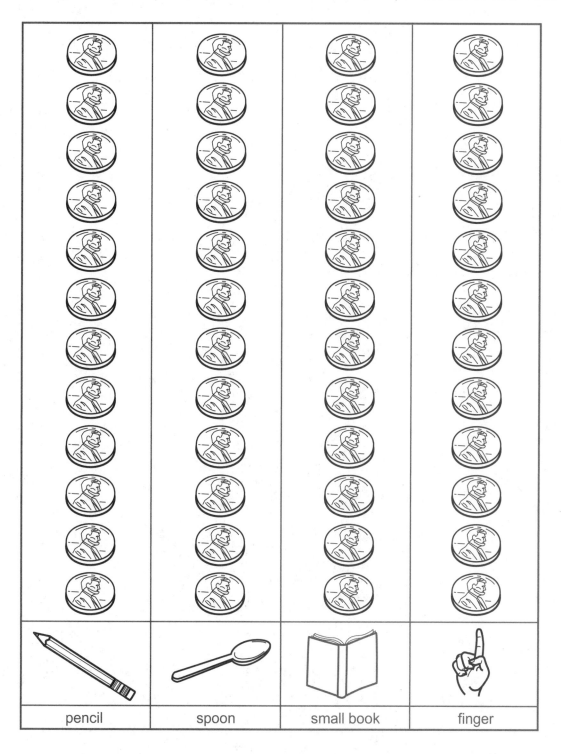

| pencil | spoon | small book | finger |

Lesson Assessment

Give Me a Hand

Questions:

1. How many hands long is your leg?

2. If two people measured a pillow with their hands would they get the same answer? Why?

3. Look at the pictograph. How many hands long is the stuffed animal?

Student Guide
Lesson 3: How Heavy? How Much?

Lesson Objectives

- Sequence objects by their weight.
- Sequence objects by their capacity.

PREPARE

Approximate lesson time is 45 minutes.

Advance Preparation

- In this lesson, your student will compare the weights of different objects. Prepare several objects of varying weights and sizes for your student to compare:

- 1. Fill four paper cups with varying amounts of rice, beans, or coins. Leave the fifth cup empty.

- 2. Test to make sure that there is a noticeable weight difference between the cups.

- 3. Cover the cups with aluminum foil and tape the edges so the contents won't spill.

- 4. Make an aluminum foil ball that is larger than the fruit you have chosen to use in the investigation.

Materials

For the Student

      bag, brown paper, lunch

      bags, brown paper grocery

      food - canned (8)

      book

      beans, dried - 3 cups

      cup, paper (5)

      foil, aluminum

      fruits - apple or orange

      index cards, 4" x 6" - numbered 1-5 (5)

      stapler

      tape, clear

Optional

    rice - uncooked, 3 cups

      How Heavy? How Much?

    cooking equipment - basin or bowl

    containers - 3 sizes (3)

    pitcher

    water

    household items - different weights (3)

    measuring cup - different sizes (3)

    cooking equipment - different containers (3)

Keywords and Pronunciation

capacity : The maximum amount of material a container can hold. A bucket has a greater capacity than a drinking glass.

weight : The measure of how heavy an object is. The largest elephant had the greatest weight.

LEARN
Activity 1: Fill 'Er Up *(Online)*

Activity 2: How Much Does It Weigh? *(Online)*

Activity 3: How Much Can It Hold? *(Online)*

Activity 4. Optional: Hold It! *(Online)*

ASSESS

Lesson Assessment: How Heavy? How Much? (*Online*)

Sit with an adult so that they may review the assessment questions with you.

LEARN
Activity 5. Optional: Estimation *(Online)*

Name _____　　Date _____

How Much Can it Hold?

In each drawing, circle the one that can hold more.

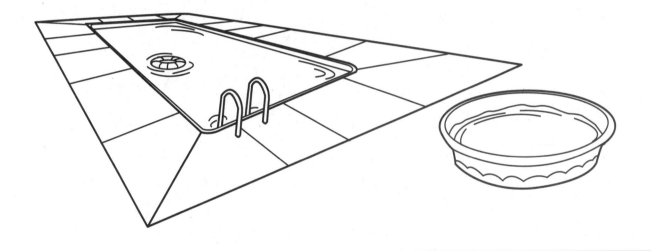

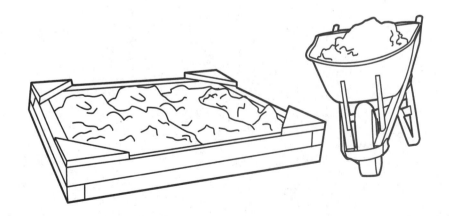

Name _____   Date _____

Lesson Assessment

How Heavy? How Much?

Part 1

This assessment is based on the *How Much Does It Weigh?* and *How Much Can It Hold?* activities. Review your student's responses on the activities and input the results online.

1. **Prepare**

   Fill four paper cups with varying amounts of rice, beans, or coins. Leave the fifth cup empty.
   2. Test to make sure that there is a noticeable weight difference between the cups.
   3. Cover the cups with aluminum foil and tape the edges so the contents won't spill.

   Investigate

   1. Let your student sequence the five index cards, numbered from one to five, on the table in front of her.
   2. Show your student the five paper cups you filled before the lesson and tell her to pick up two cups, one in each hand, until she finds the lightest cup.
   3. Ask your student to place the lightest cup on card number one.
   4. Have your student continue to compare the weights of the remaining cups and order them from lightest to heaviest on the cards in front of her. The lightest cup should be on card number one and the heaviest on card number five.

2. **Prepare**

   1. Show your student three different sized containers and discuss that sometimes it isn't easy to tell which container has the biggest capacity. Let your student examine the three containers for a minute.

   Investigate

   1. Have your student choose the container he thinks will hold the least amount and fill it with water.
   2. Ask your student to pour the water from the first container into another one. If the water does not fill up the second container, help your student understand that the first container holds less water than the second. If the water overflowed, help your student understand that the first container holds more water than the second.
   3. Have your student continue to compare how much each container holds, and ask him to order them from smallest to largest capacity.

Part 2

1. Which is heavier, a rock or a feather?

2. Which is lighter, a car or a bicycle?

3. Which holds more water, a bucket or a cup?

4. Which holds less water, a swimming pool or a bathtub?

Student Guide
Lesson 4: Hot and Cold

Lesson Objectives

- Identify household objects as being hot, warm, or cold.
- Use a thermometer to see how high and low temperatures affect it.

PREPARE

Approximate lesson time is 45 minutes.

Materials

For the Student

    crayons, 16 or more

    cups, plastic (3)

    ice cubes

    paper, 8 1/2" x 11"

    water

    thermometer - Celsius

Optional

    Hot or Cold?

    thermometer

Keywords and Pronunciation

cold : Having a low temperature. The refrigerator keeps food cold.

hot : Having a high temperature. The sunshine can be very hot on a summer day.

temperature : How hot or cold something is. The temperature of the water is very low.

thermometer : A scientific instrument used to measure temperature. The weatherman uses a thermometer to find out what the temperature is outside.

LEARN
Activity 1: What's the Temperature? *(Online)*

Activity 2: Hot or Cold? *(Online)*
Safety

Use caution when touching hot objects. Your student will be touching various items around the house; make sure that he does not touch anything that will burn his fingers.

Activity 3: Going Up *(Online)*

Safety

Do not use a mercury thermometer for science lessons. Caution your student to be careful when handling the thermometer. The glass at the bulb is very thin and could break.

Activity 4. Optional: Red Hot Review *(Online)*

ASSESS

Lesson Assessment: Hot and Cold (*Online*)

Sit with an adult so that they may review the assessment questions with you.

LEARN

Activity 5. Optional: Reading a Thermometer *(Online)*

Name _____   Date _____

Hot or Cold?

Color the hot items red and the cold items blue.

Name _____   Date _____

Lesson Assessment

Hot and Cold

Part 1

This assessment is based on the *Hot or Cold?* activity. Review your student's responses on the activity and input the results online.

Prepare

Fill three cups--one with water and ice, one with room-temperature water, and one with warm water. Place the cups on the table in random order.

1. Have your student feel the outer surface of the cups. Ask him if he feels a difference in their temperatures.
2. Now have your student dip his fingers into the water and tell you which is hot, warm, or cold.
3. Ask your student to put the cups in order from hottest to coldest.

Keep the cups of water for the next activity.

Part 2

1. What do we use to measure temperature?

2. In which direction does the red liquid in the thermometer move when it is in or near something cold: up or down?

3. What happens to the red liquid inside the thermometer when it is in or near something warm?

Student Guide
Lesson 1: Solids

Explore matter by finding examples of solids, liquids, and gases. Examine solids and liquids to find out which will sink and which will float. Freeze a liquid to make a tasty solid treat. Observe a solid change to a liquid, and then back to a solid again.

Lesson Objectives

- Observe that everything is made of matter.
- Identify solid forms of matter.
- Know that matter is a solid, a liquid, or a gas.

PREPARE

Approximate lesson time is 45 minutes.

Materials

    For the Student

        Super Solids Search Lab Sheet

        container, plastic 1 liter   - with cover

        glasses, drinking - 2 different shapes (2)

        marker, black permanent, non-toxic

        rock

        paper - sticky labels

        water - in transparent glass

    Optional

        Which Things are Solids?

LEARN
Activity 1: What's the Matter? *(Online)*

Activity 2: It's a Solid Matter *(Online)*

Activity 3. Optional: Know Your Solids *(Online)*

ASSESS

Lesson Assessment: Solids (*Online*)

You will complete an offline assessment covering the main objectives of this lesson. Your learning coach will score this assessment.

LEARN

Activity 4. Optional: Solids Sort (*Online*)

Name _____

Date _____

Super Solids Search Lab Sheet

Look around you and find solids that match the descriptions listed below. Draw a picture of the solid named in each box of the chart.

a soft solid	a hard solid	a green solid	a red solid	a solid that cannot bend
	a solid that could break if dropped	a solid that would bounce if dropped	a heavy solid	a light solid
a solid that is bendable				

Name _____   Date _____

Which Things Are Solids?

Color in the solids. A solid holds its shape.

Lesson Assessment

Solids

Questions:

1. What is everything made of?

2. What are the three forms of matter?

3. Name three things in the room that are examples of solid matter.

Student Guide
Lesson 2: Liquids

Lesson Objectives

- Test whether certain materials are liquid or solid.
- Recognize that liquids can be poured and take the shape of their containers.
- Identify liquid forms of matter.

PREPARE

Approximate lesson time is 45 minutes.

Materials

For the Student

    rock

    glass, drinking - large and small

        Does It Change Shape? Lab Sheet

    ball, rubber - small

    cotton balls

    food - honey and ketchup

    fruit drink

    milk

    plastic container - various sizes (4)

    quarters

    vegetable oil

    cup - different sizes (4)

    food coloring

    glass, drinking - short

    measuring cup

    paper - crumpled

    water

        Liquids Observation Game

Optional

    bottle, plastic

LEARN
Activity 1: A New Kind of Matter *(Online)*

Activity 2: Can You Pour It? *(Online)*

Activity 3. Optional: Solve the Riddle *(Online)*

ASSESS
Lesson Assessment: Liquids (*Online*)

You will complete an offline assessment covering the main objectives of this lesson. Your learning coach will score this assessment.

LEARN
Activity 4. Optional: Liquid Observation Game *(Online)*

Name _____   Date _____

Does It Change Shape?

Place each item in a container. Pour it into another container. Circle the results.

item	liquid (changes shape)	solid (doesn't change shape)
milk		
ball		
juice		
ketchup		
paper		
honey		
dish soap		
quarter		
cottonball		
cooking oil		

Name _____ Date _____

Lesson Assessment

Liquids

Questions:

1. Can a liquid be poured?

2. Look at the picture. What shape will the liquid take when it is poured into the container?

3. Name three examples of liquids.

4. Which can be poured and will take the shape of its container.

A.   B.   C.

5. What makes a liquid different from a solid?

Name

Date

Liquids Observation Game

Tilt the bottle of water. Color the bottles to show what the water looks like when you turn it.

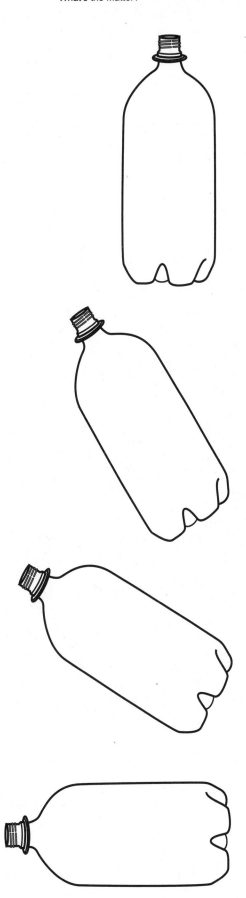

Student Guide
Lesson 3: Gases

Lesson Objectives

- Identify some characteristics of gases.
- Demonstrate that gases, such as air, take up space.

PREPARE

Approximate lesson time is 45 minutes.

Materials

For the Student

> bottle, plastic - 1 liter, empty (2)
>
> cleaning items - sink or dishpan
>
> marker, black permanent, non-toxic
>
> plastic sandwich bags, zipper-closed
>
> straws, drinking
>
> paper - sticky labels (3)
>
> water

Optional

> glasses, drinking
>
> pan, baking - shallow
>
> balloon
>
>> Is It a Solid, a Liquid, or a Gas?
>
> "Air is All Around You" by Franklyn M. Branley

Keywords and Pronunciation

gas : Matter that does not have a definite shape but takes the shape of its container, and fills up all the space in its container. A liquid, like water, can fill a glass partway, but gases, such as air, fill the entire glass.

LEARN
Activity 1: Air Is All Around *(Online)*

Activity 2: Does Air Take up Space? *(Online)*

Safety

Supervise your student closely when he uses the plastic bag. Be sure he does not place the bag over his head, or around his mouth or nose.

Activity 3. Optional: Gases Review *(Online)*

ASSESS

Lesson Assessment: Gases (*Online*)

You will complete an offline assessment covering the main objectives of this lesson. Your learning coach will score this assessment.

LEARN

Activity 4. Optional: Read About Air *(Online)*

Name

Date

Is It a Solid, a Liquid, or a Gas?

Circle the solid.

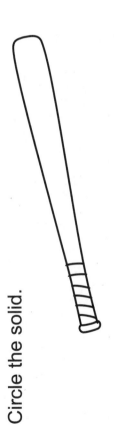

Circle the liquid.

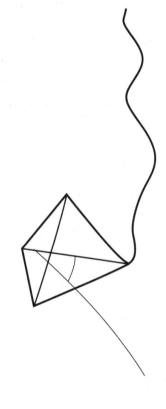

Circle the gas.

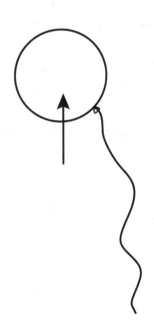

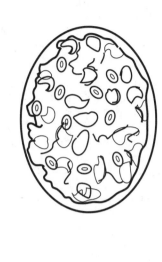

Name _____ Date _____

Lesson Assessment

Gases

Answers:

1. What form of matter is air, solids, liquids, or gas?

2. In the first investigation, why did the bag grow larger when you blew air into it?

3. Why can't you place a label or stick a note on a gas?

Student Guide
Lesson 4: Sink or Float

Lesson Objectives

- Observe that some objects sink when you place them in water.
- Observe that some objects float when you place them in water.
- Observe that one liquid can float on top of another.

PREPARE

Approximate lesson time is 45 minutes.

Advance Preparation

- For this lesson you will need to mix a small amount of corn syrup (3-4 tablespoons) with a drop or two of food coloring. Before the lesson, assemble the objects to test for sinking or floating and put them in a plastic bag. If you wish, you may use a Styrofoam packing peanut in place of a piece of a Styrofoam cup.

Materials

For the Student

    clay - 1" diameter ball

    corn syrup - 3 to 4 tablespoons

    crayons, 16 or more - one crayon

    eraser, Pink Pearl

    food - carrot or carrot piece

    nickel

    plastic sandwich bags, zipper-closed

    seeds, sunflower

    straws, drinking - small cut

    vegetable oil - 3 to 4 tablespoons

    vegetables - 1 carrot

    bowl - large and deep

    candle - birthday

    cup - styrofoam, in pieces

    food coloring

    household items - screw

    spoon - measuring

    towels, paper

    water

Optional

    Sink or Float

    foil, aluminum

Keywords and Pronunciation

predict : To say what you think will happen in an experiment. A person planting tomato seeds may *predict* that they will grow into large tomato plants.

LEARN
Activity 1: That Sinking Feeling *(Online)*

Activity 2: Sinkers and Floaters *(Online)*

Activity 3. Optional: Things that Sink or Float *(Online)*

ASSESS
Lesson Assessment: Sink or Float (*Online*)

You will complete an offline assessment covering the main objectives of this lesson. Your learning coach will score this assessment.

LEARN
Activity 4. Optional: Just Floating Along *(Online)*

Name

Date

Sink or Float

Draw each item either floating on the water or resting on the bottom of the fishbowl to show whether it sinks or floats.

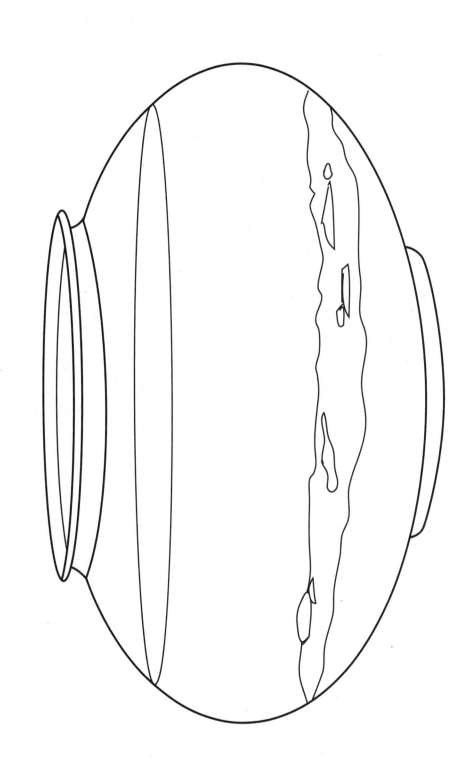

Lesson Assessment

Sink or Float

Questions:

1. Name three objects you tested that sank when you placed them in the water.

2. Name three objects you tested that floated when you placed them in water.

3. Can some liquids float on water?

4. Can some liquids sink in water?

Student Guide
Lesson 5: Changing Matter

Lesson Objectives

- Know that a liquid can change to a solid.
- Know that a solid can change to a liquid.
- Know that matter can change forms.

PREPARE

Approximate lesson time is 45 minutes.

Materials

For the Student

    butter - 2 tablespoons

    fruit drink

    plates, paper - for pouring wax on

    saucepan - for heating butter

    candle, votive

    glass, drinking

    household items - dishes; ice cube tray

    ice cubes

    matches

    plastic wrap

    toothpicks (12)

Optional

    chocolate chips

       Presto Change-O!

    plastic sandwich bags, zipper-closed

    borax

    Elmer's Glue-All

    food coloring

    water

LEARN
Activity 1: Forms of Matter (Online)

Activity 2: Matter Changes Form *(Online)*
Safety
Keep your student a safe distance from any open flames. Make sure the melted wax and melted butter are completely cool before you handle them.

Activity 3. Optional: Presto Change-O! *(Online)*

ASSESS
Lesson Assessment: Changing Matter (*Online*)
You will complete an offline assessment covering the main objectives of this lesson. Your learning coach will score this assessment.

LEARN
Activity 4. Optional: Magical Goop *(Online)*

Name _____   Date _____

Presto Change-o!

Name _____ Date _____

Lesson Assessment

Changing Matter

Questions:

1. Look at the picture. Does this picture show a liquid changing to a solid or a solid changing to a liquid?

2. Look at the picture of the ice cube tray. Does this picture show a gas changing to a solid or a liquid changing to a solid?

3. What would happen to a crayon if you left it in the hot sun?

Answer Keys

Lesson Assessment Answer Key
Observing My World

Answers:

1. observing
2. The five senses are sight, sound, taste, touch and smell.
3. Answers will vary but may include words such as rough, sharp, smooth, cold or hard.

Lesson Assessment Answer Key

A Closer Look

Answers:

1. Answers may vary, but should include the fact that your student uses his eyes to observe things or to look at things.
2. Answers may vary, but should include the fact that your student needs light to see.
3. Answers may vary, but should include the fact that items look larger with a magnifying glass than they do without a magnifying glass.

Lesson Assessment Answer Key

Sort by Sight

Answers:

1. Accept any reasonable answer that describes the toy, such as soft, smooth, fuzzy, red, or round.
2. Your student should describe some of his own features.
3. Answers will vary. Accept any reasonable answers.
4. Your student should answer that he grouped the objects into all round, brown, and long things.

Lesson Assessment Answer Key

Hear Here

Answers:

1. Your student should point to his ears.
2. Accept any appropriate answer
3. Acceptable answers may include but are not limited to these: a scream, whistle, police siren, fire alarm.
4. Accept any appropriate answer (a whisper, lullaby, cat purring, low pitched instrument).
5. Answers may vary but could include loud screaming, a fire alarm, loud music.

Lesson Assessment Answer Key

Something Smells

Answers:

1. Your student should point to his nose.
2. Your student should answer that each item has its own odor. Our sense of smell can be used to help identify unknown items.
3. Your student should answer that odor can travel through the air.
4. Answers will vary according to your student's preferences.

Lesson Assessment Answer Key

You've Got Taste

Answers:

1. taste buds
2. Your student should say that they let you experience taste.
3. Accept appropriate answers such as: sweet foods may include candy, sugar, donuts, chocolate. Sour foods may include pickles, lemons, or vinegar.
4. Your student should answer that each food has its own taste. Our sense of taste helps us identify unknown food items.

Lesson Assessment Answer Key

A Touchy Subject

Answers:

1. Answers may vary but could include a smooth pillow, shirt, table, or plastic toy.
2. Answers may vary but could include a bumpy linoleum floor, brick fireplace, or a stucco wall.
3. touch
4. the sense of sight and the sense of hearing
5. Your student should answer that each item has its own texture. Our sense of touch can be used to help identify unknown items.

Lesson Assessment Answer Key

Everybody's Bodies

Answers:

1. Answers will vary, but may include: two eyes, two arms, two legs, and so on.
2. Answers will vary, but may include hair or eye color, height, weight, and so on.
3. Answers might include eyes, ears, and mouth.

Lesson Assessment Answer Key

Bones Make Our bodies

Answers:

1. joints
2. a joint
3. skeleton
4. Bones protect the insides of our bodies.
5. your skeleton (or bones)

Lesson Assessment Answer Key

Inside Out

Answers:

1.) Your student should point to her head. Answers will vary, but should include that the brain controls the body and allows us to think and remember.

2.) It pumps blood through the body.

3.) Answers will vary, but should include that muscles move your body by pulling on the bones.

Lesson Assessment Answer Key

A Toothy Grin

Answers:

1.) to bite off pieces of food

2.) to chew and grind our food

3.) eat healthy foods, brush and floss your teeth, and visit the dentist twice a year

4.) No, the baby teeth will fall out and adult teeth will come in.

5.) sweet or sugary foods

6.)

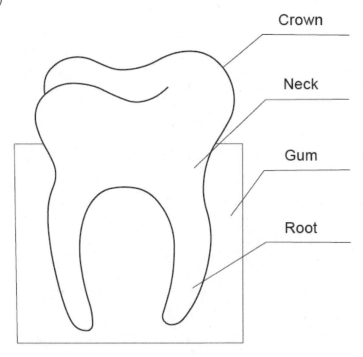

Name _____ Date _____

Lesson Assessment Answer Key

What's Alive?

Answers:

1.) living things

2.) Answers should include: Does it need food? Does it need water? Does it need air? Can it grow or move all by itself?

3.) A rock is nonliving. Answers will vary, but may include that it does not need food, water, or air and does not move by itself.

4.) An elephant is living. Answers will vary, but may include that it needs food, water, and air and can move by itself.

5.) yes

Lesson Assessment Answer Key

What Do Plants Need?

Answers:

1. They need sunlight to make their own food.
2. Plants need food, water, and air.
3. through tiny holes on the back of their leaves
4. roots

Lesson Assessment Answer Key

What Do Animals Need?

Answers:

1. food, water, and air
2. No, animals must eat plants and/or other animals.
3. Answers may vary, but should include that a shelter helps keep animals safe.
4. Animals must move to find food. They can fly, swim, and run.

Name _____   Date _____

Lesson Assessment Answer Key

Changes

Answers:

1. Accept any reasonable answer.
2. Accept any reasonable answer.
3. no

Name

Date

Plant Structures Assessment

Color the stem of the tomato plant green. Color the roots of each plant green. Color the roots of each plant brown. Color the leaves of each plant green. Color the fruit of each plant red. Color the trunk and branches of the apple tree gray.

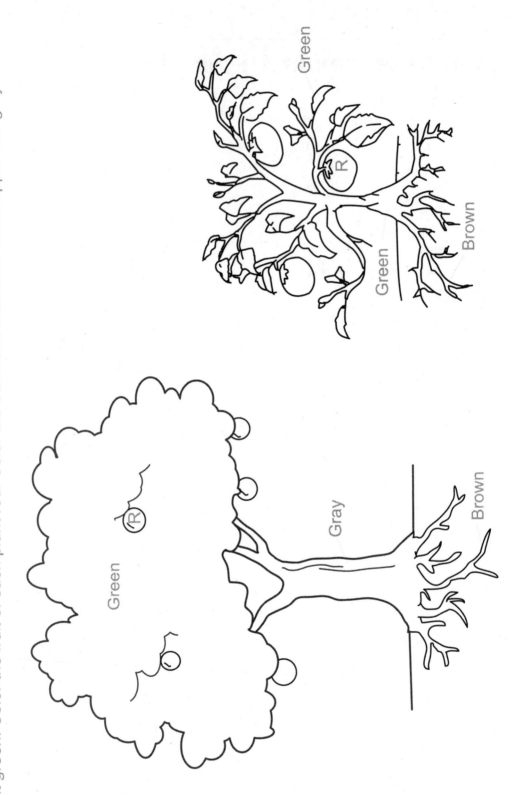

Lesson Assessment Answer Key

Sow Many Seeds!

Questions:

1. Seeds differ in size, color, shape, weight, and so on.
2. the fruit
3. Answers will vary, but may include corn, peas, pomegranates, and sunflower seeds.

Lesson Assessment Answer Key

Plants as Food

Answers:

1.) Acceptable answers may include but are not limited to a fruit such as orange, apple, grapefruit, banana, etc.

2.) Answers may vary but could include a carrot, beet, radish, or turnip.

3.) Answers will vary but could include: lettuce, spinach, broccoli.

4.) Answers will vary but could include broccoli and cauliflower.

5.) Answers will vary but could include celery, broccoli.

Lesson Assessment Answer Key

Trees Are Plants Too!

Answers:

1. deciduous trees
2. evergreen trees
3. Your student should have drawn and identified the root, trunk, branch, twig, leaf, and bark of a tree.
4. bark

Lesson Assessment Answer Key

What's That Animal?

Answers:

1.) Answers may vary but could include bear, cat, dog, sheep.

2.) a bird

3.) a worm

4.) scales

5.) a hard outer shell

Lesson Assessment Answer Key

Animal Motion

Answers:

1.) Answers will vary. Acceptable answers are dogs, human, cat, frogs, lizards and so on.

2.) Answers will vary. Acceptable answers are fish, humans, whales, dolphins, turtles, and so on.

3.) Answers will vary. Acceptable answers are birds, insects, and bats.

4.) Answers will vary. Body parts would be wings (birds), legs (frog or dogs), tail fins (fish), muscles and bones (snake), and so on.

5.) Answers will vary. Examples of body parts would be legs, wings, and tail fins.

Lesson Assessment Answer Key

What Do Animals Eat?

Answers:

1. leaves, plants

2. other animals

3. plants and animals

4. no

5. long neck and tongue

6. sharp, long claws

7. long trunk

Lesson Assessment Answer Key

Jane Goodall

Answers:

1.) Jane Goodall

2.) She saw them digging for termites with sticks.

3.) animal behavior

Name _____   Date _____

What Doesn't Belong?

Draw an X on the things that don't belong in a tree.

Name _____   Date _____

What Doesn't Belong?

Draw an X on the things that don't belong in a pond.

<u>Name</u>   <u>Date</u>

What Doesn't Belong?

Draw an X on the things that don't belong in a cave.

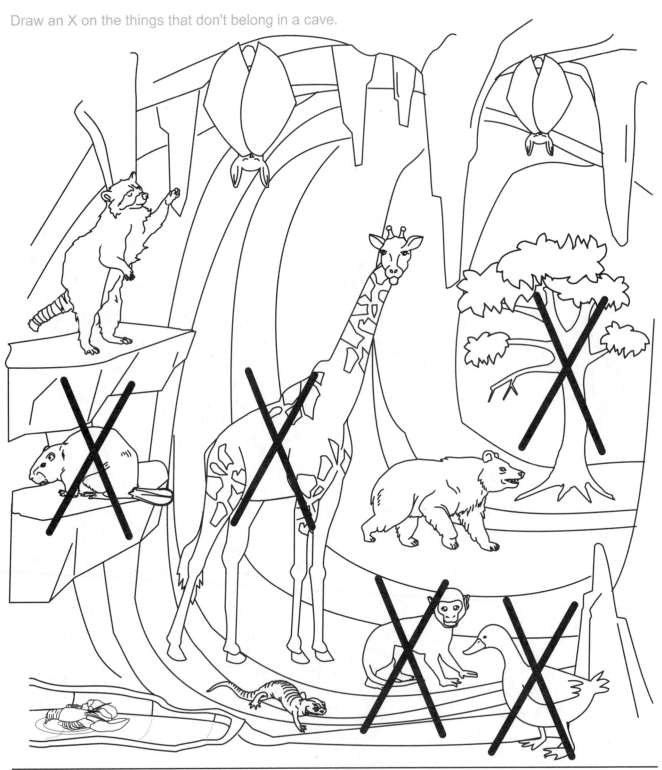

Lesson Assessment Answer Key

Length and Height

Answers:

1. Answers will vary.

2. Answers will vary.

3. a mountain

4. an arm

5. Answers will vary.

6. Answers will vary.

Name _____ Date _____

Lesson Assessment Answer Key

Give Me a Hand

Answers:

1. Answers will vary.

2. No, because people have different sized hands.

3. Answers will vary.

Lesson Assessment Answer Key

How Heavy? How Much?

Part 1

Answers:

1. Review your student's answers to the *How Much Does It Weigh?* activity. Did the student answer correctly?

2. Review your student's answers to the *How Much Does It Hold?* activity. Did the student answer correctly?

Part 2

Answers:

1. a rock
2. a bicycle
3. a bucket
4. a bathtub

Lesson Assessment Answer Key

Hot and Cold

Part 1

Answers:

Review your student's answers to the *Hot or Cold?* activity. Did the student answer correctly?

Part 2

Answers:

1. a thermometer

2. The red liquid inside the thermometer moves down the tube when something is cold.

3. The red liquid inside the thermometer moves up the tube when something is warm.

Name _____ Date _____

Lesson Assessment Answer Key

Solids

Answers:

1. matter

2. solid, liquid, and gas

3. Be sure that your student names a solid such as the rock or any object in the room that is not a liquid or gas.

Lesson Assessment Answer Key

Liquids

Answers:

1. yes

2. Round, the liquid takes the shape of its container.

3. Answers will vary.

4. B. (the honey)

5. A liquid can be poured, and it takes the shape of its container.

Lesson Assessment Answer Key

Gases

Answers:

1. gas

2. Answers may vary, but should include that air filled the bag and air takes up space.

3. Answers will vary, but should include that most gases are invisible and have no definite shape.

Lesson Assessment Answer Key

Sink or Float

Answers:

1. Answers will vary.

2. Answers will vary.

3. yes

4. yes

Lesson Assessment Answer Key

Changing Matter

Answers:

1. The picture of the icicle melting shows a solid changing to a liquid.

2. The water in the ice cube tray is changing from a liquid to a solid.

3. It would change from a solid to a liquid.